PLANNING PUBLIC SPENDING IN THE UK

GRAHAME WALSHE

MACMILLAN
EDUCATION

First published 1987

Published by
MACMILLAN EDUCATION LTD
Houndmills, Basingstoke, Hampshire RG21 2XS
and London
Companies and representatives
throughout the world

Printed in Great Britain by
Camelot Press Ltd, Southampton

British Library Cataloguing in Publication Data
Walshe, Grahame
Planning public spending in the UK.
1. Finance, Public—Great Britain
I. Title
336.4   HJ1001
ISBN 0–333–44372–1 (hardcover) ✓
ISBN 0–333–44373–X (paperback)

PLANNING PUBLIC SPENDING
IN THE UK

Other books by Grahame Walshe

International Monetary Reform
Mergers and Concentration in British Industry
  (with P. E. Hart and M. A. Utton)
Recent Trends in Monopoly in Great Britain

To John

Contents

List of Tables and Figures   viii
Preface   x
Acknowledgements   xi

Introduction: The Importance of Public Expenditure   1

1   From Plowden to Cash Planning   5

2   The Public Expenditure Planning Process   13

3   Public Spending Documentation   23

4   The Role of the Treasury   36

5   Resource Planning   48

6   The Advent of Cash Planning   59

7   A Perspective on Cash Planning   71

In Conclusion: The Future   81

Annex 1: The Definition of Public Expenditure   87
Annex 2: Cost–Benefit Studies in the Public Sector   96
Glossary of Terms and Acronyms   102
Notes and References   107
Index   120

List of Tables and Figures

Tables

3.1 1986 Autumn Statement on public expenditure   24
3.2 Public spending in cash terms by departments   26
3.3 Public spending in real terms by departments   27
3.4 1985/86: a sequence of sources for the planning total   35
4.1 Percentage changes in departmental spending between 1978/79 and 1985/86 (real terms)   38
5.1 Possible use of resources 1967/72 (basic case)   52
5.2 The growth and use of resources *1974–79*   54
5.3 Real resources available for public expenditure 1983/88   55
6.1 The Medium Term Financial Strategy: projections and outturns   69
7.1 Public expenditure plans and outturns   72
7.2 The planning total in PEWP real terms 1981/82 to 1986/87   74
7.3 A comparison between deflators   77
7.4 The planning total in real terms   78
7.5 A constellation of GDP-related objectives   79
A.1 Measures of public spending (in cash)   90
A.2 Measures of public spending (in real terms)   90
A.3 Definitions of debt interest payments (cash)   91
A.4 Measures of public expenditure as a percentage of GDP   92
A.5 The link between the three definitions of public expenditure   93
A.6 The financing of general government expenditure   94

Figures

3.1 Relationship between public spending plans and the supply estimates for 1986/87   32

4.1 Panel A: stylised budget allocations, unadjusted optimality   46

Panel B: stylised budget allocations, adjusted optimality   47

Preface

Books on public expenditure have a forbidding image. They are often written from an unacceptably partisan viewpoint; or weighed down by theoretical considerations; or remote from the institutional setting; or are highly condensed official presentations. But public spending is not the arcane subject those limitations define it to be. So in this book I have tried to reach beyond the small group of people in the City, Parliament and research institutions who make up the usual audience for material on public expenditure. My aim was to make the subject more accessible and stimulating to students of public finance and administration. I have sought to be as brief as possible; the political dimension is largely omitted; and I have attempted to simplify the theory required to give the facts their proper resonance. Four people, besides my editor Jennifer Pegg, have helped me: Anthea West, a tireless searcher after solecism; Sharon Wood, who patiently processed the typescript; David Miner, who taught me a bit about money; and David Heald, who made helpful comments on a draft. I am very grateful for their labour on my behalf.

GRAHAME WALSHE

Acknowledgements

The authors and publishers wish to thank the following who have kindly given permission for the use of copyright material:

Basil Blackwell Ltd for material from 'Public expenditure on the social services: the economic and political constraints' by G. Davies and D. Piachaud from *The Future of Welfare*, ed. R. Klein and M. O'Higgins, 1985.

The Controller of Her Majesty's Stationery Office for Crown copyright material.

Every effort has been made to trace all the copy-right holders, but if any have been inadvertently overlooked the publishers will be pleased to make the necessary arrangement at the first opportunity.

Introduction: The Importance of Public Expenditure

Media coverage of the planning and controlling of public spending in Britain is dominated by:

- the share of public expenditure in economic activity;
- the rate of growth of public expenditure;
- the tax and borrowing implications of forecast public expenditure;
- and the functional composition of spending.

By far the greater amount of attention is paid to public spending as a proportion of national economic activity, or Gross Domestic Product; and as an absolute level of spending which, because it must somehow be funded, has consequences for a range of tax and borrowing instruments.

Those are the headlines. The story behind the headlines is not less engrossing, but is infrequently told. The rest of this introduction outlines the relatively neglected themes which make up the substance of this book.

The macro economy and the micro economy

Public concern begins with macroeconomic considerations. Public expenditure can be seen as representing a large number of jobs and a great many outputs; or as pre-empting resources which would produce jobs and outputs in the private sector; or, finally, as catalysing activity in the private sector, and hence expanding the amount of resources, in particular labour and entrepreneurial ability, available for the creation of jobs and outputs. These direct and indirect effects on activity also have implications for inflation and the external sector.

Second, the microeconomic impacts are more or less salutary. Personal and company taxation, direct and indirect, will change as the result of the financing requirements flowing from spending decisions. The opportunities for consumption and saving facing individuals will be influenced both by taxation and borrowing programmes. The composition of public and private goods and services available to consumers is directly affected by government spending.

These macro and micro effects are not marginal, because public spending is a relatively large component of economic activity. Direct current and capital spending by Government on goods and services accounts for just under one quarter of Gross Domestic Product (GDP); if financial transfers are included in the definition of public spending this ratio rises to over 40 per cent of GDP; further redefinitions result in an already significant ratio expanding towards 50 per cent.[1]

However, these statistical constructs can deflect interest away from the economist's proper concern with public spending. The denominator in such ratios measures a flow of output produced and absorbed during a year. The numerator employed to provide an impression of the importance of public expenditure in economic activity has nothing to do with output. Public spending measures an input of resources. As a matter of statistical convention the output from those inputs is not measured in the national accounts. What appears as the output of the public sector in estimates of GDP is simply the sum of inputs. There are sound reasons for adopting this approach to a very difficult measurement problem.[2] But given the unknowns involved it is improper to deploy public spending/GDP ratios in arguments concerning the macroeconomic impact of the public sector.[3]

Nevertheless, public spending does represent resource use. That is the key to understanding why it is of significance in economic debate. The resources employed in the public sector could be employed to obtain valuable outputs in the private sector of the economy; or the current disposition of resources in the public sector could be reallocated to produce an alternative pattern of goods and services which would be differently valued by society. Public sector resource use thus has an *opportunity cost*. How the public sector seeks to minimise such opportunity costs, or fore-gone opportunities to obtain greater value, is the concern of this book.[4]

Public sector resource allocation

In the private sector the resource allocation problem has a market solution. Typically, the entrepreneur will be operating in an oligopolistic environment, with a modicum of domestic or international competition making the choice of price and output quantity problematic. Price and profit information is fed to decision-makers who then act to confirm or alter the existing distribution of resources. The public sector is, in contrast, the sole supplier of a multi-product line, with very patchy market information on desirable prices and quantities. How the public sector has evolved a planning process to assimilate and react to the changing pattern of perceived demands and needs is the first concern of the following chapters.

A brief history is required to gain a perspective on the planning process. That is tackled in Chapter 1, while the solution to the resource allocation problem in the public sector, a protracted bidding or auction process, is described in Chapter 2. The process is punctuated by a series of published documents which inform Parliament and the public about the latest spending decisions. Other documents comment on the decisions taken by Government or seek to explain the mechanics of the system. These constitute a valuable body of planning literature, the key features of which are signposted in Chapter 3.

The main elements of the resource allocation system are orchestrated by the Treasury. The Treasury does not control the public purse; that function is exercised by Parliament. Nor does the Treasury decide what shall be spent; that is ultimately a Cabinet decision. Nevertheless, the Chancellor of the Exchequer and the Chancellor's ministers present public spending decisions to Parliament and frame the requests for funds voted on by Parliament. In many other ways, too, the Treasury is the central figure in the public spending process. It might be expected, therefore, that the Treasury would have firmly held views about what kinds of spending were likely to minimise opportunity costs. Whether or not that is a well-founded expectation is discussed in Chapter 4.

Planning for the future

The process described and analysed in the first four chapters is a *planning* process. Planning is a function intrinsically to do with the future and, if the future is to be planned for, some forecast view of the economy is required. However, it is not unknown for economists and decision-makers to take different views about the predictability of the economy. If the economy is highly unpredictable, it might be supposed that economic planning should have a distinctly minimal role; and vice versa. A related point concerns the malleability of the economy, or the degree to which it may be, predictably or unpredictably, influenced by changes in economic policy instruments. Again, differences of view about this factor are not uncommon.

To the extent that there have been differences of view on these points they have been informed and underscored by different theories about the macroeconomic behaviour of the economy. These theories, in turn, have been influential in providing the framework for the planning process as it evolved in the 1960s and 1970s right up to the present day. Chapters 5 and 6 take a closer look at the links between these theories and the resultant planning frameworks in order to tease out the essential features of the current system.

As a final commentary on the current system, Chapter 7 provides some statistical materials which may be of use in assessing the aims and achievements of the planning mechanism currently operated. A concluding chapter speculates about evolution in the planning process.

1 From Plowden to Cash Planning

The present system of planning public expenditure is a conscious attempt to break away from the framework inherited by the Conservative administration in 1979. The first question to address is, therefore, how the present system came about. While the current planning mechanism is a radical departure from the old one, it is not possible to understand it outside the context of its antecedents. Thus, this chapter begins with a broad historical overview of public expenditure planning in the UK.

An overview

In the 1950s the 'Estimates System' was the only basis for planning public spending. Departments sent estimates of likely spending to the Treasury in December: these looked one year ahead, were on a cash basis, and appeared under about two thousand Departmental 'vote-headings'. The summation of these estimates in January provided the Chancellor with some idea of the necessary Budget measures.

It was possible to make a number of criticisms of this 'non-planning' régime. It failed to look at the future consequences of current spending, including funding difficulties; it left imprecise the physical volume of consumption and investment being catered for; it gave Cabinet and Parliament no feel for the overall allocative priorities actually being pursued; and it had as its focus an annual Budget dedicated to the *short term* management of demand and supply imbalances.

As a result of the recommendations in the Plowden Report, published in 1961,[1] this system was superseded. Henceforth, a planning system would look ahead at spending priorities with an overall resource constraint explicitly taken into consideration. From 1961 onwards public spending plans looked at the first and fifth year ahead, with a moving horizon as each year passed. Departmental votes and local authority spending were aggregated into functional programmes, such as that for transport, so that the broad allocative intentions of public sector spending policy could be assessed. The resources available to the public sector in the medium term were made the subject of a forecast. Finally, the data on spending was to be in constant prices so that volume, rather than cash, would be the basis of plans.

As the 1960s progressed the system was fleshed out. Spending for the years between the first and the fifth plan years was specified later in the 1960s. Most attention was devoted to year 3 when 'non-disruptive' changes of resource disposition could be envisaged. The plan tables and supporting text were made the subject of a published document for the first time in 1969.

As price inflation gathered pace during the 1970s the basic Plowden principles, that planning decisions should consider

● what the country can afford over a period of years having regard to prospective resources
● the relative importance of one kind of expenditure against another

became less binding. In particular, the constant–price, volume-planning system meant that an unforeseen increase in the price of resources did not reduce demand for them. Thus, the forces of supply and demand which apply to individuals did not affect the public sector. Also, unexpectedly high rates of inflation posed funding difficulties: fresh borrowing from money markets might take place on a falling market, leading to unacceptably high and variable interest rates.[2] The introduction of *Cash Limits* in 1976 was therefore informed by an increasing awareness of the monetary consequences of fiscal policy.

Cash limits were tacked on to the constant price planning system. Planning was still conducted in constant 'survey' prices, looking five years ahead, but for the first year cash limits were set on about 60 per cent of Estimates spending.[3] To breach the limits required specific recourse to Parliament, where a fresh case for resources had to be made out. In theory, if inflation was an actual 15 per cent rather than an expected 10 per cent, programme managers would have to squeeze volume by 5 per cent in that year. However, constant or 'survey' prices remained the focus of planning and these were revalued each planning year in line with actual inflation. New cash limits would be set on the basis of the new survey prices which validated all actual past inflation. Any volume squeeze imposed by cash limits could therefore operate only within the year, not between years.

The incoming Conservative administration of 1979 lived with this system for two years; but then, in 1981, it set in motion a radical reform of the planning process. From 1982 the cash available to finance public spending determined departmental volume plans. For *three* years ahead cash plans would be set from which, in principle, the Government would not be deflected. Within the overall framework of cash planning, cash limits for functional programmes were retained, but constant price expressions of plans were abolished. Cabinet and programme managers would determine priorities within the cash plans.

The sources

The first purpose of this section is to detail the documents heralding each turning point or change of emphasis in the above history. Second, certain technical features of the constant price system will be clarified.

1. *The Control of Public Expenditure.* This was the report of the Committee chaired by Lord Plowden (London: HMSO, Cmnd. 1432). It was released in an edited form to Parliament in 1961. The key recommendation of this path-breaking report was: 'That regular surveys should be made of public expenditure as a whole, over a period of years ahead, and in relation to prospective resources.' As noted in the previous section, such surveys would be informed by the principles of *affordability* and *prioritisation*.

2. White Papers reporting on development during the 1960s were published irregularly in 1963 (Cmnd. 2235), 1966 (Cmnd. 2915), 1968 (Cmnd. 3515) and in 1969 (Cmnd. 3936). These established the following features of the Public Expenditure Survey:

(i)   financial transfers within the public sector were excluded from public expenditure because, for example, including

7

Government grants to local authorities would entail double counting;

(ii) functional programmes would cross departmental and Governmental boundaries to group together all related activities;

(iii) each survey would contain a forward look at economic prospects, that is, resource availability.

In the early years only spending data for years 1 and 5 were specified; by 1969, however, figures for the intervening years had been inserted. Years 1 to 5 included the current year in which the survey took place; for example, the 1965 survey embraced 1965/66 through 1969/70.

3. A Treasury Green Paper, *Public Expenditure: A New Presentation* (London: HMSO, 1969, Cmnd. 4017), summarised developments in the 1960s and suggested the publication of regular White Papers for Parliamentary scrutiny prior to the Budget. It proposed:

(i) to publish data for one past year, one current year and four forward years; that is, one past year and five survey years;

(ii) to introduce the capital expenditure of nationalised industries, even though most such spending would be determined by commercial considerations;

(iii) to include projections of receipts from all sources on the basis of unchanged fiscal policies;

(iv) to separately specify direct use of resources by Government, financial transfers, and the acquisition of tangible and financial assets;

(v) to include in total outlays an allowance for the Relative Price Effect (see the Glossary and the discussion in Chapter 7).

Subsequent changes drew upon many of these proposals.

4. The White Paper, *Public Expenditure 1968/69 to 1973/74* (London: HMSO, 1969, Cmnd. 4234) was the first Public Expenditure White Paper published in the regular annual series.

5. The White Paper *The Attack on Inflation* (London: HMSO, 1975, Cmnd. 6151) was mainly concerned with the introduction and application of a prices and incomes policy. However, a section on public expenditure presaged the introduction of cash limits. It

was thought that the volume planning system needed to be sensitive to cash costs in a period of rapid inflation. Government could help counter inflation by making clear that: '... Government's purchases of goods and services will have to be cut back if prices rise too high' (paragraph 45).

6. The White Paper, *Cash Limits on Public Expenditure* (London: HMSO, 1976, Cmnd. 6440), introduced cash limits covering the 1976/77 plan year. The paper deplored the absence of a firm cash control system under volume planning. Cash limits would contribute to the attack on inflation because public sector managers would have to cut back on purchases if prices increased more rapidly than expected. The mechanism was meshed in with the constant survey prices of volume planning. To obtain cash limits one started with the 1975 survey prices of:

A Autumn 1974: these were revalued to what would become the *1976* Survey basis of...

B Autumn 1975: and these were in turn revalued to prices forecast to obtain during 1976/77 on average.

It was noted that in this sequence of revaluations moving from [A] to [B] could be performed with known data on costs and prices, while moving beyond [B] would obviously be more conjectural and might, for example, involve wishful thinking in terms of targets rather than forecasts.[4] Also, the more highly aggregated the indices used beyond [B] the more likely that, because an *average* rate of inflation was assumed to hold for all programmes, some programmes would be volume-squeezed while others would gain an unplanned increase in resources. Any volume squeeze under cash limits could be reversed in the following year by employing more realistic factors in moving beyond [B].[5]

7. The White Paper, *The Government's Expenditure Plans: 1982/83 to 1984/85* (London: HMSO, 1982, Cmnd. 8494) introduced cash planning. While retaining cash limits for approximately 60 per cent of Supply Estimates, cash planning covers the whole of the public expenditure planning total. Three broadly synchronised measures catered for the extra uncertainty involved in extending cash control over the whole of public expenditure. First, there was a larger unallocated contingency reserve which was to increase

further in subsequent years. Second, the 1980 Survey had reduced the number of plan years to three; thus, the 1981 public expenditure White Paper detailed spending for three survey or plan years, 1981/82 through 1983/84. Third, if there were exceptional movements in costs, programme managers could make proposals to adjust the cash provision. This far from automatic safety net was announced in the autumn of 1981.[6]

Because volume planning and the system of constant survey prices was abandoned, a new system of cash revaluation factors was introduced based upon assumptions about future inflation. Thus, starting from:

THE AVERAGE LEVEL OF PRICES OBTAINING in 1981/82	. . .	a cash level higher by approximately 7 per cent was decided to give . . .
THE PLANNING TOTAL OBTAINING IN 1982/83	. . .	and, in turn, a cash level higher by 6 per cent was decided to give . . .
THE PLANNING TOTAL OBTAINING IN 1983/84	. . .	and finally a cash level higher by 5 per cent was decided to give . . .

CASH PLANS FOR 1984/85

The intention was that, once set during the 1981 Survey, these revaluation factors would not be adjusted. Thus, the phenomenon under cash limits whereby volume squeezes between years could be automatically reversed by uprating survey prices in each new survey year could not occur. Any volume squeeze under year 1 of cash planning would carry through into year 2. Any squeeze in year 2 would be additional to that experienced in year 1 and *both* would be carried forward into year 3. It remained to be seen whether departments would attempt to reverse a volume squeeze experienced in the first years of cash planning. Government statements implied an unshakeable resolve to stick to firm cash plans; so, in the nature of things, it was unreasonable to expect an announcement about possible ground rules concerning that potential problem.

Cash planning: Some early views

It is interesting to close with three contrasting views concerning the advent of cash planning. The Chancellor of the Exchequer thought that cash planning: '... will change the framework of decisions, and is seen as a major contribution to improving financial management, supporting the other efforts being made to increase cost consciousness and accountability throughout the public sector'.[8] Elsewhere, commentators interpreted the statements of ministers and departmental officials as indicating that: 'It was to bring home to Departments and unions the trade-off between wage increases and jobs that the recession and a non-expansionist economic policy had forced upon the private sector'.[9]

Finally, David Heald took the view that cash planning was likely to lead to volume cuts:

> Cash planning makes revaluation shortfalls cumulative in their impact. Revaluation only takes place at the predetermined cash limit factors. The method through which major volume cuts can be secured is quite clear: the revaluation factors set in the 1982 White Paper (Cmnd. 8494) indicate that this is likely to happen unless they are, in the event, revised.[10]

At least two of these views have a political dimension which the following chapters eschew. An evaluation of what cash planning has actually achieved in the way of volume change will be held over until Chapter 7.

Summary

The three phases of public expenditure planning since the Plowden report (volume planning, volume planning with cash limits, and cash limits with cash planning) have been informed throughout by the basic Plowden principle of affordability. Once it became clear that that principle was imperfectly served by the old survey price system, the Government instituted cash control procedures of increasing rigour. These were ostensibly intended to place cash availabilities before the volume plans espoused by departments and achieved a shift of emphasis away from planning towards control.

2 The Public Expenditure Planning Process

The planning of public expenditure is subject to a fairly tight timetable of key dates when major decisions are taken about:

● the overall level of public expenditure;
● the distribution of spending between programmes;
● the communication of plans to Parliament.

In theory, each of these three decisions is constrained by the timetable to take place at, or no later than, a specific date; but in practice the planning process ensures that all three areas are more or less continuously under review. Moreover, the cycle for one planning year overlaps that for the preceding and following years.

The timetable for a specimen planning year is given below. It is depicted as starting at the beginning of the calendar year and continuing up to the following January. Adjustments for temporal realism will be introduced in the following section.

Period	Event
January	Top management in each department starts to review departmental aims and objectives, activities and resources; output measures and performance indicators are contrasted with planned targets. Intra-departmental adjustments to the cash baseline and functional distribution are proposed in the light of that review. The Treasury circulates to departments the latest forecasts of prices, unemployment and interest rates to allow those with significant demand-led spending to plan

realistically. Treasury may also offer informal guidance on the likely cash revaluation factor to adopt for the creation of year 3 plans.

February   The assessment of objectives and performance continues. Departmental finance divisions formally ask for divisional cash bids for plan years 1, 2 and 3. Non-finance divisions are putting together the numbers and texts describing what the cash is to be used for.

February/March   Departmental finance divisions receive bids and contrast plan years 1 and 2 with years 2 and 3[1] from the previous survey to establish divisions seeking:

● Additional Bids
● Reduced Requirements[2]

Meanwhile, following Cabinet discussion and decision, Treasury guidance is received by departments on how the survey is to be conducted. This covers such matters as the baseline (which may involve recent switches within and between departments); the new plan year 3 which is derived from the old plan year 3, plus a revaluation factor reflecting an allowance for higher prices; how and when additional bids and reduced requirements will be incorporated into the survey; and the description of outputs, which may include a review of value for money in a selection of departments.

March/April   Departmental finance divisions communicate the results of the initial data collection to top management and ministers. The Budget will give rise to new data to feed into econometric forecasts of prices, unemployment and interest rates. Details of the subsequent Treasury post-Budget assumptions are fed to departments. The baseline numbers and texts covering programme outputs are communicated to Treasury in April.

April   Each department finalises its baseline report, which Treasury will aggregate into the Survey baseline report.

May   To make room for bids for additional resources, and in the event that an overall reduction in resources is decided by Cabinet, departments are sometimes asked to provide data on those activities it is possible to cut. These *Options for Reductions*, agreed by departmental ministers, are put to the Treasury. Departments and Treasury explore these options at an official level. The Treasury may propose specific reductions and discuss the costing of these options with departmental officials. Then, in late May, departmental ministers write to the Chief Secretary to the Treasury listing and ranking bids for additional resources over and above the baseline.

June   Cabinet members receive the PES Report from Treasury.

July   Several papers drawn together by Treasury officials are discussed in Cabinet: (i) the PES Report drawing together departmental spending plans; (ii) the Chancellor's report on prospects for the macro economy. This includes how much overall growth there is likely to be and, therefore, the resources likely to be available for private plus public consumption and investment; the outlook for prices, unemployment, and the external sector; and, most importantly, how the cash

15

sums in departmental spending proposals relate to prospective monetary developments over the medium term; (iii) an outline of additional bids for resources. Cabinet makes a decision about the overall spending limit in the light of these papers. *Usually* this spending limit will be less than the sum total of departmental bids.

End-July   The Chief Secretary to the Treasury writes to departments pointing out the discrepancy between the planning total limit decided by Cabinet and the aggregate of departmental spending plans. The Chief Secretary puts outline proposals to departments on where they might usefully make room for additional resource bids. Departmental ministers and officials consider their strategy for the forthcoming bilateral discussions with the Treasury, when the proposed 'cut' will be discussed.

September   'Bilaterals' commence. Departments either settle or disagree with the Chief Secretary to the Treasury after protracted negotiations spreading over two or three meetings.

September/October An upper tier of bilaterals is possible where unresolved issues are put to the *Ministerial Group on Public Expenditure*, chaired by a senior Cabinet member without departmental responsibility (since its inception in 1981 the Chairman has been Lord Whitelaw). This so-called 'Star Chamber' is comprised of: the Chairman, the Chief Secretary to the Treasury, and two or three other departmental ministers who have already settled and who have no conflict of interest with their own spending plans. Thus, the composition of the Star Chamber can change at different sittings and between years.[3]

November	If this second tier bilateral fails to resolve the dispute a minister may seek a 'trilateral' with the Prime Minister or, exceptionally, take the issue to full Cabinet where a final decision is taken. This Cabinet, on the first or second Thursday in November hears from the Chancellor the results of the Chief Secretary's labours to get within the agreed July total. Following the Cabinet meeting the Autumn Statement is made to Parliament. This includes the public expenditure planning total for years 1, 2 and 3 and the individual programme totals at a high level of aggregation. It also includes a forecast for the macro economy which the Government is required to publish twice a year under the provisions of the Industry Act 1975. Departments prepare detailed tables and texts for inclusion in the White Paper.
December	Departments provide texts and tables to Treasury for the Public Expenditure White Paper (PEWP).
January	The PEWP is published covering years 1, 2 and 3. The next planning cycle starts in departments.

Timing variations

The first point to make about the above narrative is that individual departments do not necessarily stick rigidly to that timetable. Increasingly, departments are recognising that if the work put into assessing objectives, resources and outputs is to have a practical influence on the bidding process then results need to be to hand earlier than January or February.[4] Moreover, ministers will be involved in discussing these reviews not simply because of the significant implications for spending plans but also because of the need to learn their lines for bilaterals later in the year. Ministerial involvement, which is especially required for input on the precise weighting to give to (possibly conflicting) objectives, is clearly continuous rather than spasmodic.

At the other end of the timetable the White Paper may occasionally be published later than January. One motive for early publication is to give the House of Commons Treasury and Civil Service Select Committee sufficient opportunity to discuss and comment on the argument and presentation of the White Paper before the Budget and detailed spending proposals are debated in Parliament. However, a rapidly changing policy situation affecting a few departments will upset the aspiration to publish early with firm figures. Publication has sometimes been as late as Budget time.[5] Thus there are pressures to stretch out the timetable at both ends.

Local authorities, whose spending is part of public expenditure, work to a slightly different timetable. In an effort to influence the budget-making activities of local authorities the Government now gives the local authority sector as a whole an indication of the Government grant it is likely to receive in the following financial year by July. Each local authority can then plan the overall make-up of its budget during July through November. In mid or late December individual authorities receive data on their desired spending levels and grants, together with information about the likely grant penalties, if any, for exceeding the desired spending levels. From 1985, also, selected local authorities have had limits set to their rate poundages such that their two main sources of finance, government grants and rates, are virtually constrained to the spending limit announced in December. The budget-making and rate-setting activity of local authorities after December, and prior to the publication of budgets and rate poundages in the spring, is much occupied with contentious marginal adjustments to the service composition of the budget, or with ways and means, including creative accounting, whereby such adjustments may be minimised.[6] For public expenditure purposes local authority spending is included in departmental totals, even though it may be subject to very little departmental control. Thus, the sum of all authorities spending plans announced in December is constrained to fall within the departmental totals announced earlier in the Autumn Statement.

The External Financing Limits (EFLs) of the nationalised industries – covering their market and overseas borrowing, the value of leased assets, and grants and subsidies from central government – are included in the definition of public expenditure (see Annex 1). Normally, EFLs are agreed during the bilaterals in time for the Autumn Statement. However, because they depend ultimately upon revenue and costs stretching some eighteen months ahead they are often subject to change during the course of the first plan year. There is also a facility whereby industries can exceed their limit for one year at the expense of the following year's limit.[7] These arrangements, comprising less than 2 per cent of public spending, take up an inordinate amount of ministerial and Cabinet time. They are something of a special case, however, and will not be discussed further.

Adversarial planning

There are several schools of thought concerning departmental strategies in discussions about options for reduction and additional bids. One takes the view that Departments offer 'bleeding stumps' for Treasury officials to weep over.[8] A 'bleeding stump' does not necessarily mean an activity that has already been cut to the bone. Thus, Department of Energy ministers and officials may wish to explore the implications of cuts in the Redundant Mineworkers Payment Scheme. Because this spending programme is politically sensitive, and Cabinet would feel very exposed were it to be reduced in real terms, the department goes into the bilaterals with a strong hand.

That kind of scenario is now unrealistic. The expansion of White Paper details concerning departmental activities, feeding as it does on the supply of texts from departments themselves (see below, Chapter 3), and the presence in the Treasury of expenditure divisions whose main function is to shadow the activities of particular spending departments, provide the Treasury with a degree of countervailing power. Hence, it is simply not possible to distort bilateral negotiations by including on the agenda only a select list of irreducible items.

An alternative view is that departments are quite open about the actual potential for cuts across the whole range of their activities, detailing precisely where one, two, five or even ten per cent savings on resources are possible given reduced commitments, or relaxed timetables, or resource-saving capital investment. In a world where ministers are rated according to their relative ability to command resources such a view is also untenable. As Ponting has observed:

> If the minister is trying to maximise his budget the worst tactic he can adopt is to try and negotiate reasonably. In 1975 Fred Mulley (Secretary of State for Education) agreed a cut of £580 million in his bilateral with the Treasury. Encouraged by this success, the Treasury promptly reneged on the agreement and demanded another £124 million in savings. As Mulley complained to the Cabinet, 'those who offered the most were penalised the most'.[9]

The most likely strategy pursued by departments is one where activities which are genuinely thought to contain some scope for input reduction, or which the department holds to be of less value in achieving its objectives, are offered up – *but with something in reserve*. This protects real bleeding stumps and what may be described as 'high marginal value' programmes. It also retains some room for manoeuvre should the prospects for spending suddenly worsen during the first planning year, the end of which lies some twenty months ahead. The financial pressures placed on departments by the introduction of cash ceilings have undoubtedly added to the incentive to increase their negotiating margins. Finally, the interposition of the Star Chamber in the bargaining process will have swelled such 'slack', as Likierman has observed: 'The greater the number of stages a programme has to pass, the greater the temptation to build in amounts which can be conceded in negotiation. It is therefore impossible to judge whether the amount bid was intended to provide an inbuilt element of slack.'[10]

In essence, then, departments and the Treasury are adversaries in the planning process. This is seen most clearly in the changed arrangements for making bids for additional resources. These are now the subject of a separate bidding letter by each departmental minister at the end of May. Prior to 1986, bids for additional resources surfaced from the departmental bidding process with the finance division and ministers acting as little more than providers of gloss and post boxes between departmental divisions and the Treasury. These aggregated bids would be agonised over for months, whittled away by a process of argument, counter-argument and denial until by the autumn a position near the baseline was arrived at. Next year the same grinding routine would start again with a familiar line-up of additional bid candidates dusted down and presented for inspection.[11]

The Treasury might be forgiven for seeing that as a debilitating and resource-wasting exercise rather than as a necessary part of the process whereby relative priorities gradually emerge. The presentation of baseline plus additional bids as an aggregated departmental bid and, therefore, a kind of baseline, meant that efforts to reduce the additional bids could be spoken of as 'cuts'. That would be seen as bad public relations by any Government.

The new arrangements whereby departmental ministers must keep apart the departmental bidding process and routine baseline reporting can be viewed in one of two ways. In the spirit of adversarial planning it may be seen as a pre-emptive strike by the Treasury; a 'cut' before 'the cuts'. Under the changed circumstances PESC[12] does not get notice of how each department is bidding. Thus a channel whereby departmental officials could report back to their ministers on the 'tone' of extra-departmental bidding has been disrupted. This *may* reinforce the tendency to prune the list of additional bids under the new arrangements, so as not to be seen to be risibly out of line in the July Cabinet.

Or it may, on the other hand, mean that the new system will lead to more entrenched attitudes. Under the system of late summer bilaterals there is considerable ignorance, after July, of just what is being conceded by other departments. Thus departments naturally wish to concede as little as possible. The changed arrangements of 1986 may tend to sharpen the bilateral nature of the planning process and serve to weaken the already limited element of multilaterality inherent in the system. It is still too early to say whether the new system actually makes it more difficult for the Treasury to deliver the agreed Cabinet spending total.

It is clear that the role of the Treasury in the whole planning process is pivotal between departments and Cabinet. Such an important function in the PES process requires separate consideration. This will be held over until Chapter 4.

21

Summary

At the outset of this chapter it was stated that the PES process decides the level and relative shares of public expenditure between departments. In terms of timing, the basic level of public spending is decided in July although subsequent tinkering with the composition of spending can continue right up until the Budget in the following spring. The actual process of bargaining which takes place in the PES is best described as 'adversarial planning' and it remains to be seen whether changes introduced in 1986 modify that picture.

3 Public Spending Documentation

The planning of public spending in Britain is brought to the attention of the public by a series of published documents. Most of this literature is constitutional in the sense that it signifies the Government (the Executive) informing Parliament (the Legislature) about decisions which require Parliamentary sanction. It is also part and parcel of the business of ordering spending priorities to the extent that Parliamentary debate informs spending plans. Hence, familiarity with the published sources is indispensable for a full understanding of the planning process.

The Autumn Statement (AS)

Publication of the AS is usually attributed to a recommendation in a report from the Institute for Fiscal Studies, the Armstrong Report.[1] It was first published in 1982, although prior to that date the Chancellor made a statement to Parliament in the autumn detailing prospects for the economy and giving expenditure plans.

Much of the AS is given over to a one-year-ahead review of the economy: domestic activity, inflation, the labour market, the external sector, and the financial markets as they might be affected by fiscal developments. This leads naturally into a consideration of public spending plans in years 1 through 3. As may be seen from Table 3.1, programme detail is minimal, although there are separate prose texts concerning the nationalised industries, the local authorities and prospects for the privatisation programme. The AS is concluded by short chapters on national insurance contributions and the revenue effects of illustrative tax changes. It therefore stops short of integrating spending plans with funding decisions. The latter are, of course, the subject of the Budget in the spring.

Table 3.1 *1986 Autumn statement on public expenditure*

Departments (including local authority spending and nationalised industries' external finance)	Estimated outturn	New plans		£000s
	1986/87	1987/88	1988/89	1989/90
Ministry of Defence	18600	18790	18980	19470
FCO—Diplomatic wing	670	700	730	750
FCO—ODA	1320	1360	1400	1440
European Communities	1090	870	440	1060
IBAP and other CAP expenditure	1520	1660	1780	1880
Domestic agriculture, fisheries and food	920	880	900	900
Forestry Commission	50	50	50	60
Department of Trade and Industry	1370	1110	960	950
Export Credits Guarantee Department	250	160	110	50
Department of Energy	170	−90	−50	−250
Department of Employment[24]	3970	4050	4240	4340
Department of Transport	4920	5140	5080	5140
DOE—Housing	2850	3200	3020	3090
DOE—Other environmental services	4070	3850	3890	3930
DOE—Property Services Agency	−90	−90	−90	−90
Home Office	5260	5540	5700	5870
Lord Chancellor's Department	620	670	720	770
Department of Education and Science	15950	16600	17350	17840
Office of Arts and Libraries	800	810	830	860
DHSS—Health and personal social services	17960	19100	19840	20720
DHSS—Social security	44500	46000	47400	49300
Civil superannuation	1140	1240	1330	1410
Scotland	7810	7950	8100	8220
Wales	3060	3190	3300	3390
Northern Ireland	4530	4810	4980	5150
Chancellor's departments	2070	2230	2320	2420
Other departments	450	570	600	620
Privatisation proceeds	−4750	−5000	−5000	−5000
Reserve	——	3500	5500	7500
Adjustments	−700	−260	−270	−280
Planning total	**140400**	**148600**	**154200**	**161500**
General government expenditure	**164400**	**173700**	**179600**	**187800**

Note: Departmental figures are affected by substantial rounding, including the 1986/87 outturn figures to reflect their provisional nature; hence figures may not sum precisely to totals. For other notes see source.

Source: *H M Treasury Autumn Statement 1986* (London: HMSO, 1986) Cmnd. 14, Table 2.3.

The White Paper

The Public Expenditure White Paper (PEWP) appears in January or February, although in years of exceptional indecision publication has been delayed until the Budget. First publication in the current form dates from 1969. Currently, there are two volumes. The first is a summary and introduction where the plans are set out in the following ways:

● in cash terms;
● in aggregate terms for 5 past years, the current year and 3 plan years;
● by department for 2 past years, the current year and 3 plan years.

The first volume distinguishes between spending by planning authorities (central government, local authorities and public corporations), spending by economic category (pay, goods and services, financial transfers, and so on) and spending by departmental interest. At the end of Volume I, a few paragraphs on Civil Service manpower and running costs focus on a component of public spending which is thought to be of some public concern.

Since the advent of cash planning the PEWP has consistently fought shy of constant price volume series for spending either in Volume I or II. In a minor concession to persistent criticism[2] of this perceived deficiency the 1985 PEWP included what was called a 'real terms' planning total. By this was meant the cash figures in the PEWP, given here in Table 3.2, deflated by past and expected changes in the *GDP deflator*. Thus, for example, taking 1986/87 estimated outturn cash of £140.4 billions, and assuming the GDP deflator to advance by 2.8 per cent during 1986/87 (from the 1985/86 base), there is a 'real terms' 1985/86 basis expenditure of:

$$\frac{£140.4}{1.028} = £136.5 \text{ billions in } 1985/86 \text{ prices}$$

which is the figure appearing under 1986/87 in the PEWP real terms table (appearing here as Table 3.3)[3].

An obvious question to ask is: how relevant is the GDP deflator in tracing developments in the prices of labour, goods and services and other economic categories in public spending? Gross Dom-

Table 3.2 *Public spending in cash terms by departments*[1]

£billion

Departments	1984/85 outturn	1985/86 outturn	1986/87 estimated outturn	1987/88 plans	1988/89 plans	1989/90 plans
Defence	17.2	18.0	18.6	18.8	19.0	19.5
Foreign & Commonwealth Office	1.8	1.8	2.0	2.1	2.1'	2.2
European Communities	1.0	0.8	1.1	0.9	0.4	1.1
Ministry of Agriculture, Fisheries and Food	2.0	2.4	1.9	2.3	2.4	2.5
Trade and Industry	2.1	1.8	1.6	1.3	1.1	1.0
Energy	2.6	0.7	0.2	−0.1	−	−0.2
Employment	3.1	3.4	3.9	4.0	4.2	4.3
Transport	4.6	4.6	4.9	5.1	5.1	5.1
DOE—Housing	3.3	2.8	2.8	3.2	3.0	3.1
DOE—Other environmental services	4.0	3.9	4.1	3.8	3.9	3.9
Home Office	5.1	5.3	5.9	6.2	6.4	6.6
Education and Science	14.0	14.5	16.0	16.6	17.4	17.8
Arts and Libraries	0.7	0.7	0.8	0.8	0.8	0.9
DHSS—Health and personal social services	15.8	16.6	18.0	19.1	19.9	20.8
DHSS—Social security	38.1	41.5	44.5	46.0	47.5	49.3
Scotland	7.0	7.2	7.8	8.0	8.1	8.2
Wales	2.6	2.8	3.0	3.2	3.3	3.4
Northern Ireland	4.1	4.3	4.7	4.9	5.1	5.2
Chancellor's departments	1.7	1.8	2.1	2.2	2.3	2.4
Other departments	1.2	1.2	1.5	1.7	1.8	1.9
Reserve				3.5	5.5	7.5
Privatisation proceeds	−2.1	−2.7	−4.8	−5.0	−5.0	−5.0
Adjustment[2]			−0.2			
Planning total[3]	129.8	133.6	140.4	148.6	154.2	161.5
General government gross debt interest	16.1	17.7	17.5	18.0	18.0	19.0
Other national accounts adjustments	4.2	7.2	6.5	7.0	7.5	7.5
General government expenditure[3]	150.0	158.5	164.4	173.7	179.6	187.8

[1]Figures rounded to £0.1 billion except for the forward year figures for general government gross debt interest, which is rounded to the nearest £1 billion and other national accounts adjustments which are rounded to the nearest £½ billion. This table includes all spending on departmental policies, whether through central government, local authorities or public corporations.

[2]An adjustment for the difference between the assessment of the likely outturn for 1986/87 and the sum of the other items shown, plus an allowance for the external finance of those nationalised industries being privatised during that year.

[3]Totals have been rounded independently.

Source: H M Treasury *The Government's Expenditure Plans 1987/88 to 1989/90* (London: HMSO, 1987) Cmnd. 56–I, Table 1.6, p. 12.

Table 3.3 *Public spending in real terms by departments*

£billion

Departments	1984/85 outturn	1985/86 outturn	(base year 1985/86) 1986/87 estimated outturn	1987/88 ᵢplans	1988/89 plans	1989/90 plans
Defence	18.2	18.0	18.1	17.6	17.2	17.1
Foreign Office	1.9	1.8	1.9	1.9	1.9	1.9
European Communities	1.0	0.8	1.1	0.8	0.4	0.9
Ministry of Agriculture, Fisheries and Food	2.1	2.4	1.9	2.1	2.2	2.2
Trade and Industry	2.2	1.8	1.6	1.2	1.0	0.9
Energy	2.7	0.7	0.2	−0.1		−0.2
Employment	3.3	3.4	3.8	3.8	3.8	3.8
Transport	4.9	4.6	4.8	4.8	4.6	4.5
DOE—Housing	3.4	2.8	2.7	3.0	2.7	2.7
DOE—Other environmental services	4.2	3.9	4.0	3.6	3.5	3.5
Home Office	5.4	5.3	5.7	5.8	5.8	5.8
Education and Science	14.8	14.5	15.5	15.6	15.7	15.7
Arts and Libraries	0.7	0.7	0.8	0.8	0.8	0.8
DHSS—Health and personal social services	16.7	16.6	17.5	17.9	18.0	18.3
DHSS—Social security	40.4	41.5	43.2	43.1	43.0	43.4
Scotland	7.5	7.2	7.6	7.5	7.3	7.2
Wales	2.8	2.8	2.9	3.0	3.0	3.0
Northern Ireland	4.3	4.3	4.5	4.6	4.6	4.6
Chancellor's departments	1.8	1.8	2.0	2.1	2.1	2.1
Other departments	1.2	1.2	1.5	1.6	1.7	1.7
Reserve				3.3	5.0	6.6
Privatisation proceeds	−2.3	−2.7	−4.6	−4.7	−4.5	−4.4
Adjustment			−0.1			
Planning total	137.6	133.6	136.5	139.3	139.7	142.1
General government gross debt interest	17.0	17.7	17.0	17.0	16.0	16.0
Other national accounts adjustments	4.4	7.2	6.5	6.5	6.5	6.5
General government expenditure	159.0	158.5	159.9	162.8	162.7	165.2

Source: H M Treasury, Cmnd. 56–I, Table 1.8, p. 17.

estic Product, as the name implies, embraces all activity in the domestic economy, both private and public consumption and investment activities (with exports minus imports also added).[4] It may well be irrelevant for the purposes of tracking the volume of public spending over time because a public spending price deflator may be systematically different from the GDP deflator.

A 1986 report by the National Audit Office (NAO) clarifies the issues here.[5] 'Volume' may mean the following:

- cash figures of spending with the effect of inflation removed by the GDP deflator;
- cash figures of spending with the effect of inflation removed using price indices specific to the activity concerned;
- physical output measures.

Diagrammatically:

Constant price measures		Real volume
Real or cost terms — Using GDP deflator	Volume — Using specific indices	Direct Physical Measures

All three measures have their uses. The NAO suggests that there may be greater scope for the use of constant price volume series, in particular where direct physical measures cannot be aggregated to give an impression of service provision.[6] Constant price volume series using specific price indices are resisted by the Treasury for a variety of reasons:

(i)   they may be used as a misleading proxy for the level of service or output;
(ii) programme managers may use them, with target input levels, to derive cash entitlements;
(iii) they undermine the philosophy of cash planning whereby cash provision remains invariant to unanticipated changes in inflation.

There is no question, however, that when measuring the true volume of resource inputs specific activity price indices are clearly superior to the GDP deflator.

Volume II of the PEWP gives a more detailed account of the overall figures found in Volume I. Apart from special sections on nationalised industries and local authorities, it is mainly devoted to separate departmental chapters, starting with defence. These narratives tell us more about what resources are actually spent on. In recent years there have been many attempts to develop output measures and proxy output measures ('performance indicators') as the main material for the departmental chapters. It is reasonable to suppose that this development received fresh impetus from the Financial Management Initiative, although many departments would no doubt claim that work on output measures was in hand in any case.

As the departmental chapters progressively improve their accounts of outputs produced the absence of relevant input volume is more acutely felt. The 'indicators of output', actual measures of output or, most tentatively, 'examples of partial indicators of intermediate output'[7] are in direct or physical terms. However, the input data elsewhere are in cash terms. Consequently, it is not possible to match up the two so that input-output relationships may be, however approximately, inferred. There are exceptions to this rule. For example, in the transport chapter for 1986, it is possible to contrast a constant price series for current expenditure on road construction, improvement and maintenance with data on route miles constructed and renewed.[8] The impartial observer may well ask that if this analysis is possible for roads might it not also be possible for, say, certain aspects of work in the National Health Service or the criminal justice system?

The second volume of the PEWP is, finally, notable for the *Explanatory and Technical Notes*. The 1986 introduction to these notes contains a lucid and succinct description of what is accomplished by the PES. But it belongs at the beginning of Volume I rather than at the back of Volume II:

● The system of annual surveys for planning public spending over the next few years has developed over the last 25 years. During the Survey the Government decides both what the total of public spending should be and how that total should be allocated between different departments. The allocation reflects past commitments and the Government's priorities for public spending.[9]

Financial Statement and Budget Report (FSBR)

This report, published at the time of the Budget, updates the AS and PEWP but also introduces the revenue side of the account. It has already been noted that the AS includes a final short chapter on the 'revenue effects of illustrative tax changes'. These are merely stylised numbers which do not commit the Government to any actual tax changes. Nor do they indicate proposals for tax changes. The FSBR, therefore, is the first published document in the PES cycle to show how the spending proposals might be paid for in terms of actual instruments. It is true that one intermediate target of the Medium Term Financial Strategy (MTFS) is the limit to cash borrowing, from which it must follow, because public spending is financed either by tax receipts or borrowing, that taxation falls out as a 'planned residual'. However, the relative neglect of the funding picture by the AS has attracted much criticism.[10] It can be argued that if the Government does not specify which tax instruments are to bear the burden of tax gathering, then the realism of implied taxation targets cannot be assessed; and, hence, the realism of borrowing targets cannot be assessed. Thus, in the absence of specified tax targets by instrument, money markets must make best guesses, using the AS information on cash spending targets and illustrative tax yields. All of this may add to general uncertainty making the Government's funding problems more acute and, perhaps, raising the costs of debt funding above the level otherwise obtainable.[11] Presumably the Government does not take such arguments very seriously, because it has retained the historic practice whereby tax changes are announced at Budget time. *Not* announcing tax changes six months before the Budget also reduces the number of representations made to the Chancellor by the various interest groups predicted to suffer.

Apart from updating those parts of the AS to do with macroeconomic prospects, public spending, and national insurance contributions, the FSBR also rolls forward the MTFS and sets out in great detail the public sector financial transactions which led to the borrowing figure in the MTFS.

Summary and Guide to the Supply Estimates (SGSE)

This little-known document is published at the same time as the FSBR. It provides the link between the PES planning system and the Estimates System, by which most of the cash required for public spending is voted in Parliament. The links between public spending and cash voted in Estimates is seen with the aid of a diagram taken from the SGSE.

The main point to note is that a significant proportion of public spending is financed by contributions from the National Insurance Fund (in turn partly funded by wage and salary earners) and the rents and rates collected by local authorities – neither of which involve Parliamentary sanction. Thus, in the plan year 1986/87, £99 billions out of £139 billions, or getting on for three-quarters of the planning total, was subject to Parliamentary approval in Main Estimates.[12]

Reports of the Treasury and Civil Service Committee

These are not Government documents relating to the PES round; yet they are of sufficient importance to be noted here. Since the turn of the 1970s the House of Commons, Treasury and Civil Service Committee, an all-party body, has reported on the White Paper and, since 1982, on the Autumn Statement. Among their chief concerns have been presentation, changes in definition which affect the interpretation of spending trends, and the basis for comparisons of input/output relationships over time and between departments.

However, they range somewhat wider than that description implies. In the 1985 report on the PEWP, for example, it was pointed out that for the nationalised industries to achieve their External Financing Limits (EFLs) it was likely that they ' . . . will resort to using their monopolistic power to raise prices'.[13] Again, in their comments on the 1986 Autumn Statement most attention was devoted to the conduct of macroeconomic policy, and in particular monetary policy, rather than to the public spending issues raised by the AS.[14]

Their main and persistent criticism of Government reports on plans has been the absence of an account of how spending

Figure 3.1 *Relationship between public spending plans and the supply estimates for 1986/87*

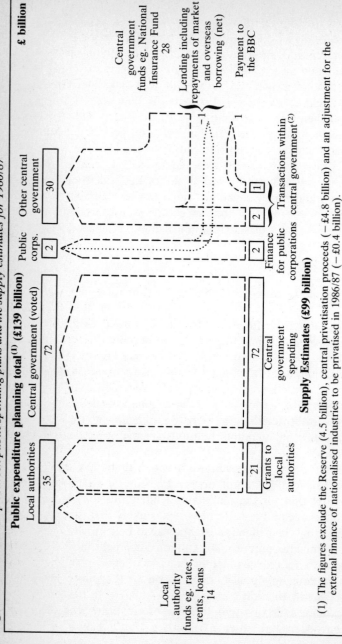

(1) The figures exclude the Reserve (4.5 billion), central privatisation proceeds (−£4.8 billion) and an adjustment for the external finance of nationalised industries to be privatised in 1986/87 (−£0.4 billion).

(2) This covers transfers within central government (£2.4 billion), for example, the 'Treasury Supplement' to the National Insurance Fund (class XV, vote 6), and a payment (£1.0 billion) to the BBC in respect of licence revenue (class XI, vote 4).

Source: H M Treasury *Supply Estimates 1986/87, Summary and Guide* (London: HMSO, 1986)

priorities are ultimately determined. In 1986, for example, the Committee were sceptical about the degree to which the PEWP plans were the outcome of an informed and unconstrained Cabinet debate concerning priorities for spending. The Committee took the view that the nature of PES deliberations is essentially bilateral (Treasury–Department) rather than multilateral (in Cabinet):

> We have the impression, however, that agreements reached *bilaterally* between the Treasury and spending Departments are unlikely to be challenged at any stage in the process. As a result, it must be impossible for the Cabinet, in arriving at its final decision, to look across the board at a potential ordering of priorities different from that reached in individual nego- tiations.[15]

Other documents

These, then, are the main published documents in the PES cycle. There are unpublished documents which are seen by PESC and Cabinet, most notably the PES Report to Cabinet in July. Although it is intended to be very secret, the most interesting and important details of the latter are invariably leaked to the media. In particular, the difference between the summed bids from departments for the first plan year, and the figure for the same year appearing as plan year 2 in the PEWP of the preceding January, is usually given much prominence.[16]

Occasionally, the Government publishes a public spending paper of wider significance than those which set out plans for the next three years; for example, the Green Paper on taxation possibilities over the medium to long term.[17] This Green Paper assessed the probable trend rate of GDP growth and assumed a path for public spending as a proportion of GDP. Together with a projection of debt interest payments this gave the amounts required to be financed by taxes (broadly defined to include national insurance contributions and rates) and borrowing. Taking North Sea oil tax revenues and public sector borrowing as given it was therefore possible to derive the non-North Sea oil tax-take as a residual. It transpired that if public spending was projected to remain constant up to 1989 non-North Sea oil taxes could be reduced below the level inherited by the Conservative administration of 1979 – to about one third of GDP.

The Green Paper was thus of vital significance to the debate on public spending. It showed that, as well as a commitment to planning in cash terms, the Government framed high level quantitative objectives which integrated spending, borrowing and taxation targets. It was rather odd that this novel approach should be consigned to the relative obscurity of a Green Paper which has excited little Parliamentary interest. Nevertheless, elements of the target framework constantly appear in the AS, the PEWP and the FSBR. Chapter 7 attempts to assess the current status of this approach.

Finally, this chapter would be incomplete without a reference to proposed reforms of PES documentation. Apart from the reforms pressed by the House of Commons select committee, radical suggestions for change are contained in a study report from the Institute of Public Sector Management at the London Business School.[18] The authors suggested:

● an expanded AS covering three years with Budgetary information enabling a comprehensive Parliamentary debate;
● scrapping the PEWP;
● a Budget document covering expenditure and its financing;
● departmental reports to come out at Budget time integrating Supply Estimate information with spending data.

These were the main changes proposed together with a number of other exhortations towards greater clarity in presentation. To date only the AS has been amended to include all three plan years rather than just one plan year.

The NAO report on Financial Reporting to Parliament covered much the same ground as the LBS paper without making similarly radical recommendations.[19] It calls for clearer statements of departmental aims and objectives and better information on how these aims and objectives are served by outputs of departments. This is seen as the basic requirement for an informed Parliamentary debate on spending priorities. But the bulk of the NAO report discusses the problem of the 'read-across' from the public spending documents to the Estimates documents scrutinised by Parliament. This issue is not unimportant, but it is beyond the scope of this book.

Summary

The AS, PEWP and FSBR constitute a rolling sequence of documents relating to PES data. Table 3.4 follows the data for the plan year 1985/86 through these documents, starting with the PEWP for January 1984. As can be seen the data does not lack change even though the entries for two of the documents (AS 1985 and PEWP 1985) are little more than confirmation of the planned spend in the FSBR.

Table 3.4   *1985/86: a sequence of sources for the planning total*

PEWP 1984	AS 1984	PEWP 1985	FSBR 1985	AS 1985	PEWP 1986	FSBR 1986	AS 1986
132.0	132.0	132.1	134.2[1]	134.2	134.2	133.9	133.6[2]

(1)   Incorporating + £2.0 billions addition to the Contingency Reserve and + £0.1 for budget measures in respect of employment and training schemes.
(2)   Latest estimated outturn.
Sources: PEWP 1984, Cmnd. 9143; AS 1984, HC12; PEWP 1985, Cmnd. 9428; FSBR 1985, HC265; AS 1985, HC22; PEWP 1986, Cmnd. 9702; FSBR 1986, HC273; AS 1986, Cmnd. 14.

4 The Role of the Treasury

On the one hand, the system of resource allocation described in the first three chapters may be seen as approaching the ideal. The cycle of events is annualised so that account may be taken of the rapidly changing economic circumstances affecting departments; the confrontation between departments and Treasury teases out the ordering of essential priorities; there are sufficient non-partisan voices in Cabinet to provide a balanced cross-departmental view of value for money; Parliament is given ample opportunity to question the use of resources; and the whole process is smoothly knitted together by the professionals in the Treasury.

On the other hand, it is possible to take the view that the system has several defects. First, the timetable ensures that Cabinet ministers are not allowed to coolly reflect on inter-departmental priorities. The PES report and associated papers arrive, at the earliest, in June for Cabinet discussion in mid-July. Then, the holiday season takes over, followed immediately by bilaterals. In the circumstances, a reasoning approach to priorities is an improbability. As Barbara Castle has observed:

> There is always an enormous waste of time over these public expenditure exercises. I spend hours mulling over this statistic and that and preparing my case, but in the end Cabinet decides these things on a kind of hunch. A bias builds up against this programme or that. If the tide is with one, one wins. Rational argument has little to do with it.[1]

Second, decisions on where to allocate extra resources will tend to be determined by the strength of the personality of ministers rather than the force of their appeal to economic and social values. A strong minister, even with the flimsiest of cases for extra resources, will be able to intimidate Cabinet colleagues with equity principles or an historic manifesto commitment. This has been forcefully put by Joel Barnett:

> Expenditure priorities were generally decided on often out-dated and ill-considered plans made in opposition, barely thought through as to their real value, and never as to their relative priority in social, socialist, industrial or economic terms. More often they were decided on the strength of a particular spending Minister, and the extent of the support he or she could get from the Prime Minister.[2]

Third, the bilateral nature of the PES process, as has been pointed out by the Treasury and Civil Service Committee (see above, Chapter 3) will tend to stifle Cabinet discussion of changing priorities. Because most ministers have arrived at deals with the Treasury before Cabinet decisions are due to be made, the debate clearly cannot be without prejudice. Moreover, the bilateral as opposed to multilateral nature of negotiations is designed to maximise the intransigence of ministers. Ultimately a minister will not wish to be seen to be losing out relative to Cabinet colleagues; and because bilaterality entails a *sequence* of negotiations over time, ministers cannot know how all deals will be concluded. Given these arrangements there will be a natural temptation to concede little, if anything at all.

It is occasionally supposed that the ordering of priorities emerging from the PES process is 'politically' determined. In this context 'political' can be taken to mean ensuring that priorities are driven by manifesto commitments.[3] Table 4.1 portrays the sort of 'before-and-after' tabulation which is used to support this view-point.[4] Thus, the predilections of the 1979/86 Conservative administrations are said to have been expressed in the increasing shares going to agriculture ('the Shires vote'), the Home Office ('Law and Order') and defence ('the nuclear deterrent').

This *post hoc ergo propter hoc* argument is unconvincing. Apart from the particular facts surrounding each departmental cash requirement – agricultural expansion was caused mainly by EC obligations, defence expansion was largely the result of a NATO commitment, the 1981 police pay formula proved unexpectedly expensive, and so on – it is clear that overriding external constraints have been very influential in fashioning the profile of changing shares observed in Table 4.1. For example, how would it have been possible *not* to increase the share of spending on employment programmes, pensions and unemployment benefit in the circumstances of the 1980s? This is not to deny that ministers have on occasion appealed to manifesto promises, nor that in one or two cases, for example law and order, there does appear to have been a very marked change in spending compared to the 1970s.

Thus a set of fairly binding (social, economic, demographic and physical) external constraints tends to inform spending priorities in the medium to long term. In the short to medium term ministers, fronting large and complex departmental organisations, attempt to beat the trends and maintain or increase their share of resources. This need not be viewed as irrational behaviour: ministers believe

Table 4.1 *Percentage changes in departmental spending between 1978/79 and 1985/86 (real terms*)*

	Percentage of planning total in 1978/79	Percentage change since 1978/79
Employment	1.6	+67
Agriculture	1.3	+63
Home Office	3.1	+41
DHSS: Social Security, etc	25.0	+34
Defence	11.4	+30
DHSS: Health & Personal Social Services	11.3	+20
Arts and Libraries	0.5	+13
Scotland, Wales & N. Ireland	11.2	+ 5
Energy	0.8	0
Education & Science	11.8	− 1
Foreign & Commonwealth/ODA	1.6	− 4
Environment	3.4	− 5
Transport	4.0	− 8
Chancellor's Department	1.7	−11
Other	1.2	−11
Housing**	5.4	−43
European Community	1.1	−43
Trade & Industry	3.6	−56

*'Real terms' here means that cash figures have been deflated by the GDP deflator. 1985/86 data have been transformed into share percentages from which the percentage change in share since 1978/79 has been derived.

**Housing figures are gross of receipts.

Source: Derived from Cmnd. 9143 and 9702.

in and in many cases can demonstrate at length the real social and economic value of their programmes. But ministers tend also to be relatively uninformed about the economic and social values arising from the programmes of other departments.

This unsatisfactory state of affairs, whereby resource planning negotiations are conducted in a state of vincible ignorance, could be improved upon if there were a strong central body capable of giving the Cabinet guidance on spending priorities. This role could be performed by the Treasury. The Treasury is the protagonist in the PES process: it drafts and issues the initial guidelines for each round of the PES under Cabinet direction; it provides the chair and secretariat for PESC; it is the channel for instructions from Cabinet to departments and to PESC; it is the seminal influence in developing the PES system in terms of presentation and technical refinement; and it has statutory powers to approve departmental Estimates, which are the means of obtaining cash from Parliament for spending plans. This book would not therefore be complete without some account of the part played by Treasury officials and ministers in the PES process of resource prioritisation.[5]

Control of the aggregates

The first Treasury interest in the PES process is that public spending is a large macroeconomic aggregate about which it is impossible not to take a view. Annex 1, on measuring public expenditure, shows that direct public spending on goods and services represents almost one quarter of Gross Domestic Product. The management of financial transfers within the community – such as pensions and unemployment benefit – represents about one fifth of GDP. These magnitudes are too important for government to ignore.

The need to make judgements about the appropriate level of public spending is not affected by fashions in economic theory concerning the optimal methods for control of the economy. Public spending might be seen as a means of purposive intervention to correct imbalances between aggregate demand and supply. This view can be dubbed the demand management school of thought. Or the fashion might be for establishing a target medium term path for the monetary aggregates, including public spending in so far as it affects money, in the expectation that this non-interventionist stance will minimise deviations from the sustainable rate of economic growth. This view has been associated with the monetarist school of thought. In either case, and those two schools of thought do not exhaust the possibilities,[6] planning and control of aggregate public spending is implied.

Priorities and value at the margin

One Treasury view is that their ministers are concerned with the aggregate of public spending and anything else is incidental.[7] But there are a number of reasons why Treasury interest should not be confined to the aggregates and why the sub-components of spending and the relative priority given to them should be given primary consideration.

First, the PES system is an incremental budgeting system concerned with marginal changes. This makes it inevitable that Treasury will become embroiled in discussions of value at the margin or, more generally, 'value for money'. Exploring value for money at the margin can be understood as a necessary condition for obtaining maximum value from a given budget. Hence, the marginal conditions for maximising value from a given cash budget: to obtain maximum total value the *marginal* value per pound spent must be equal for all goods and services purchased. If this condition does not obtain it implies that, by rearranging spending, total value can be increased.[8] The basis for a Treasury interest in marginal values should thus be clear. If Treasury argues for a cut it needs to know that it is not proposing to cut resources where they are deriving most value. Equally, if it concedes a bid for additional resources it wishes to ensure that they are destined for programmes promising the greatest returns.

The above argument is so transparently unexceptional that the reason for differences of view between Treasury and departments is not immediately obvious. However, there is scope for such disagreements. What counts as *value* in this context is not always objectively measurable. Moreover, value will be inextricably related to departmental objectives and the interpretation of departmental objectives may not be straightforward. In particular, a variety of sectional interests will be lobbying departments in

40

order to offer them interpretations of their objectives and the weights which should be given to them. Such conflict is in principle resolved by Cabinet deliberations and consensus on the pattern of values informing spending priorities. But, as we have seen, the structuring of the PES prevents the emergence of such a consensus.

Treasury also has an interest in departmental detail because of timing considerations. For example, when a decision is made to increase aggregate spending, some types of spending may be expected to feed through to increased outputs and employment in the economy more rapidly than others.[9] If, for such macroeconomic reasons, there are times when Treasury wants certain types of spending to expand at the expense of others, it is not too difficult to understand why some departments will complain that they are victims of expediency.

Does Cabinet need guidance on priorities from a Treasury equipped to provide an overall objective view? In theory, there is in Cabinet an informed discussion of the relative values to be attached to different types of spending. This need not actually be in the course of full Cabinet business. For example, the so-called 'Star Chamber' is said to act as a Cabinet sub-committee on prioritisation by custom and usage.[10] In practice, however, most members of Cabinet have a departmental interest to defend and pursue a subjective assessment of relative values.

Prioritisation in practice

How probable is it that the Treasury can orchestrate a rational discussion of relative priorities during the PES? There are at least two issues here: the capacity of Treasury officials to evaluate marginal costs and benefits; and whether or not departmental and Treasury ministers have the time or inclination to understand and debate priorities.

As regards the first of these there is patchy evidence to support the view that Treasury staffing policy in this area may at times lead to a rapid turnover of key personnel.[11] It may be that staff in expenditure divisions simply do not have the time to master the detail, often of a highly technical nature, required to understand what is being achieved by departmental resource use.

As regards the second issue, the Chancellor was once asked by a member of the Treasury and Civil Service Committee:

> Could you tell us what the machinery first of all available to Government is for comparing the relative priorities of expenditure under different departmental heads, and also tell us where those decisions are taken? . . . Who is providing the analysis so that Ministers can make judgements about the relative priority of different heads of expenditure?

The Chancellor replied: 'I do not think that the procedure can be as scientific as you imply.'[12] He went on to state that priorities were discussed in Cabinet sub-committee, bilaterals, the Star Chamber and Cabinet itself, which were all the time trying to make decisions consistent with declared manifesto policies and external constraints.

Other ex-Treasury ministers have said that they had insufficient opportunity for discussion of relative priorities. For example, during two Labour administrations, those of 1964/70 and 1974/79, there were attempts to set up Cabinet sub-committees devoted to such analysis, but both failed to establish themselves.[13] The system of reviews of spending areas which Pliatzky refers to as existing under the current Conservative administration may be an attempt to improve matters.[14] However, the fruits of such reviews need to be drawn together and it is difficult to imagine that happening without the support of a co-ordinating official body. One source from which such advice might have arisen, the Central Policy Review Staff, was abolished in 1983.[15]

There is, however, a much more fundamental question about capability. How would an objective Treasury observer know the rate at which to trade-off hospital beds against prison cells, against microcomputers in schools, against more and better roads? This question is addressed by Pliatzky who was once directly involved, at the highest level, in the Treasury handling of public expenditure issues.[16]

An answer based solely on economic theory is relatively simple. While recognising that there are technical problems of evaluation, the economist would propose that an attempt is made to assess the costs and benefits of employing resources in each departmental set of programmes. The standard prescription would be cost–benefit analysis (CBA). Pliatzky deprecates the use of CBA; it is regarded as offering little scope for choosing between priorities.[17] Nevertheless, CBA and related techniques would seem to be the only objective basis for proceeding in this difficult area.[18]

Let us recall that CBA attempts to impute shadow prices where market prices cannot be observed. Using these prices, benefit–cost ratios, and a ranking of such ratios, may be generated. The cost side in CBA poses some, but not insuperable, difficulties among non-profit making institutions in the public sector. For the most part, opportunity cost reasoning can establish useful proxies for resource costs where, as sometimes occurs, the actual market price of a resource does not reflect a wider concept of social accounting price. Real problems emerge in establishing benefits. In the terminology of CBA it is the assessment of consumer *willingness to pay* for non-marketed goods which involves many CBA studies in arcane measurement problems. Very often benefit estimates are controversial; or highly uncertain; or the measurement of benefit is not attempted with the authors relying on the argument that, since all options will yield roughly the same physical level of provision or design standard, the study resolves itself into a cost-effectiveness analysis.

Mooney has shown that where such measurement problems are vexatious they need not be intractable. Thus, if marginal costs of different health treatments are known, and it can be assumed that decision-makers have maximised returns to the budget, the implied values of the different treatments may be deduced.[19] A particularly striking example of implied value analysis cited by Mooney is contained in a study by Pearce and others of the value of a life implied by various policies in the health field.[20] The US data for this study indicated a cost per life saved of at least $110 000 with a policy of stringent environmental standards for smoke emission; whereas the marginal value of a life saved from heart disease varied between $6000 and $46 000, depending upon the treatment pursued. Davies and Metcalf give another example of this approach in the comparison of costs per job for a selection of employment-creating policies in the public sector.[21] Their article argued that Special Employment Measures (SEM) have much lower costs per job than spending on defence, health, education, and so on; in order to derive the maximum value per £

borrowed by the public sector, therefore, spending should accordingly be targetted on SEM.

There are two points to make about the very considerable body of CBA and related studies listed in Annex 2. First, these studies and other unpublished CBA work in departments could be consolidated. For each of the activities making up programmes in departments, ministers should have a summary statement of what CBA research has so far shown in terms of benefit–cost ratios. Such statements would comment on the major areas of uncertainty and on aggregation and scale problems.[22] Second, the techniques of CBA enshrined in these studies now have a long history. The procedures are well established and the crucial assumption of CBA – that data on consumer willingness to pay measures benefit – stands scrutiny. There is therefore an onus on those who would *not* support the employment of CBA and implied value analysis in government to propose a better alternative.[23]

However, how likely is it that any systematic cross-departmental comparison of value for money will be employed by ministers? That is, assuming departmental projects could be ranked by benefit–cost ratios in a format allowing departmental trade-offs to be clarified, would ministers allow such rankings to inform public spending priorities?

The issue is represented schematically in the diagram for an imaginary world of five departments. The problem is how to allocate a budget across departments in order to maximise the return to limited resources. There are a number of arguments for supposing that the actual budget distribution will depart from the 'optimal' distribution and may, in any one year, by typified by the allocation in the second diagram:

● *Uncertainty*: as the dotted lines indicate each set of ranked projects/activities will not have certain outcomes. There may be grounds for assuming that high return activities are also highly uncertain. Although Treasury advice on project selection in the public sector is that decision-makers should be 'risk neutral'[24] – on the grounds that for a large number of projects 'losers' will be roughly offset by 'winners' – the possibility that many highly risky projects are located in high return departments will tend to promote a switch away from the 'optimal' distribution.

44

- *Human error*: there may be grounds for supposing that some departments are persistently optimistic or pessimistic in their assessments of returns.
- *Strategic considerations*: these might override the prescription to invest in a high benefit–cost activity. For example, there might be a need to fund research into the methods of nuclear waste disposal (even when returns are relatively low, because they are heavily discounted) lest the coherence of the overall energy strategy is jeopardised.
- *Equity*: the returns to an activity may not be competitive in cross-departmental terms, yet considerations to do with 'fair shares' – for example to redress inner city dereliction, or to provide infrastructure in an area suffering from long term locational disadvantage – will dictate that resources are allocated non-optimally.

While such exceptions may be generally recognised, and may in an ideal setting encourage ministers and officials to attempt more systematic cross-departmental comparisons, the prospects are not promising. In an outcome such as is portrayed by Panel A of the diagram it is clear that, rigidly applied, there is only one outright winner. Most ministers would, by the rules of such a system, expect to gradually lose position in the pecking order. The outcome illustrated in Panel B is more realistic but nevertheless entails a distribution which, over the life of a Parliament, would concentrate growth in one or two well-placed departments. Hence, this stylised depiction of a well-informed bidding system ultimately shows us why there is little hope for improvements in the process of refining priorities: if ministers are risk averse by nature they will refuse to countenance such priority ordering systems.

The way out of this impasse is not clear. If the role of the Treasury was more powerful, that is, if control over priorities was the subject of greater central direction, there might be improvement. But an expanded role for the Treasury need not provide a solution. Some more imaginative institutional initiative may require consideration.

Figure 4.1 *Panel A: Stylised budget allocations unadjusted optimality*

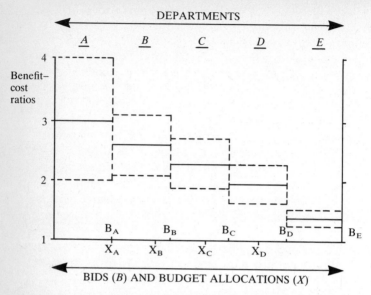

Departments offer a range of marginal projects. For example, Department A offers projects with benefit–cost ratios ranging from 1.0 to 3.0, while department B offers projects with benefit–cost ratios ranging from 1.0 to 2.6. Only the top ranking projects are shown in the diagram. Projects have uncertain outcomes. Thus, for example, department A's top-ranking projects have a range of outcomes with benefit–cost ratios of 3.0 ± 1.0. These ranges are indicated by the broken lines in the diagram. The marginal budget is £3 billions. All five departments submit bids of £1 billion. In panel A the budget allocations illustrate the optimal distribution designed to maximise returns to the budget:
$A = £1.0$ billion; $B = £0.8$ billion; $C = £0.7$ billion; $D = £0.5$ billion; E is allocated zero marginal resources.

Summary

The role of the Treasury is crucial in the PES round. Deriving its authority from an amalgam of precedent and historical and statutory sources it makes the running in the PES timetable. While its concern is chiefly with the aggregate of public spending there are sound reasons for the Treasury wishing to comprehend the detail of programmes and sub-programmes. Chiefly, in an incre-

Figure 4.1 *Panel B: Stylised budget allocations adjusted optimality*

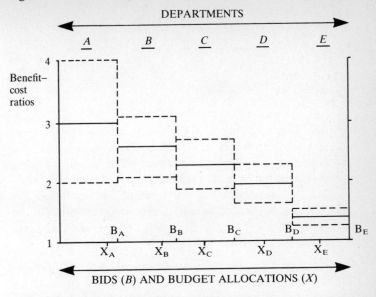

Panel *B* of the diagram has exactly the same projects offered by departments as before. The marginal budget is again £3 billions and each department submits a bid for £1 billion. However, in the budget allocation consideration of uncertainty, strategic factors and equity has allowed the actual distribution to depart from the optimal distribution:
$A = $ £0.8 billion; $B = $ £0.7 billion; $C = $ £0.5 billion; $D = $ £0.5 billion; $E = $ £0.5 billion.

mental budgetary system government ought to be seeking to obtain maximum value from limited resources. Whether in practice either Treasury officials or ministers can function efficiently at the sub-aggregate level is uncertain. They have neither the resources nor, apparently, the inclination to do so. Moreover, if they could inform a rational cross-departmental ordering of priorities it is doubtful whether their Cabinet colleagues would give them the support required to make the system work.

5 Resource Planning

This and the following chapter will develop a fresh theme. Over the last quarter of a century the PES process has evolved in the light of changing economic philosophies. The actual planning frameworks employed were thus inspired and informed by reasonably distinct theories about the management and control of the economy. In this chapter the broadly Keynesian credentials of the planning framework used in the 1960s and 1970s will be discussed. There are thus three related tasks:

- to outline the Keynesian framework of the demand management school;
- to suggest how the resource planning model grew out of that framework;
- and to place the aspirations of resource planning in the wider context of indicative planning.

The major features of the 1980s model will be held over until the next chapter.

Aggregate demand management

The planning of resource use depends upon resource availability so that in the 1960s the output growth prospects for the economy had to be determined in order to start the planning exercise. For Treasury economists nurtured in the Keynesian tradition this came naturally. Keynesians were accustomed to theorising in terms of aggregate supply and aggregate demand: supply consisting of domestic output and imports, while demand consisted of private consumption and investment demand, the current and capital spending of government, and the overseas demand for exports. Thus:

$$Y + M = C + I + G + X$$

where
- Y = domestic output
- M = imports
- C = private consumption
- I = private investment
- G = government spending
- X = exports

The Keynesian insight that equilibrium in this goods market could exist alongside disequilibrium in factor markets, particularly in the labour market where there might be substantial unemployed resources, was the key element of his theory. Keynes alleged that the Classical notion of perfectly functioning markets was unacceptable. The actual system of markets was certainly incapable of alleviating unemployment by means of changing prices and the interest rate mechanism. Market prices changed very sluggishly; and the decrease in interest rates brought on by reducing incomes would do little to stimulate investment demand. Keynes thus proposed an alternative policy: positive action by government to expand aggregate demand. This would help to overcome disequilibrium in goods and labour markets simultaneously. Hence the emphasis in Keynesian orthodoxy on aggregate demand management to achieve equilibrium in goods markets – obtaining price stability, and labour markets – to eliminate unemployment.[1]

Given the low rates of price inflation and unemployment experienced in Britain in the 1950s and 1960s[2] it was not surprising that Keynesian orthodoxy held sway. Again, with a slight rearrangement of the aggregate supply and aggregate demand equation (subtracting imports from both sides):

$$Y = C + I + G + [X - M]$$

it was possible to focus on domestic demand and a net external balance expression; thus, the essentials of the system were clear and simple to grasp. This had undoubted presentational advantages in dealing with ministers lacking a formal economics training.

The events of the late 1960s and 1970s, when inflation gathered pace at the same time as unemployment increased, posed considerable difficulties for demand management. Faced with these disequilibria the Keynesian prescription would be to both depress and expand demand simultaneously. The instruments whereby demand might be controlled, monetary and fiscal policy, also appeared to be inextricably linked. Therefore, the opportunity to use one instrument to reduce unemployment and another to curtail inflation was not available.[3] While these problems emerged on the demand side, the supply side appeared not to be as resilient as in the 1950s: the promise of expanding aggregate demand might bring forth increased prices rather than increased supply.[4]

These difficulties were sufficient to confound the prevailing orthodoxy and prepare for the advent of a different theory concerning the proper role of economic management. That development is described in the next chapter. For the present, the Keynesian ideas outlined above give the intellectual context of the planning model developed in the 1960s.

The prior claims model

The resource planning framework began, as we have seen, with an assumption concerning aggregate supply or output availability. Then, aggregate demand was partitioned into prior and secondary claims. The thinking behind the prior claims model was revealed fairly early in the 1960s:

> If the demands arising from public expenditure rise faster than the nation's production, a smaller proportion of the latter is available for exports, private investment and consumption not generated by public expenditure. In order to keep room for an adequate rate of growth of exports and private investment, it would then be necessary to restrain the growth of private consumption.[5]

These speculations appeared during the Conservative administration of 1959/64. While exports and private investment were clearly first claims on national production it was not quite clear whether public or private consumption had priority. However, there could be no doubting the ordering of priorities emerging from a White Paper published during the Labour administration of 1964/66:

50

The Department of Economic Affairs and the Treasury there-fore prepared an initial assessment of the growth of gross national product which could reasonably be expected, and then of the resources which were required to improve the balance of payments, to strengthen private and nationalised industries' investment, to provide for the expansion of public expenditure on the lines of the policies then ruling, and to allow for the growth of private consumption.[6]

Thus far the model seemed to the outside observer to consist of a few rudimentary calculations on the back of an envelope. Little explicit attention seemed to be paid to fitting private and public resource demands into an overall framework. The model was evidently employed to provide an initial grasp of the potential for the growth of public spending without committing ministers to any particular rate of public sector growth. After the sterling devalua-tion of 1967 resource planning operated in an atmosphere of crisis:

> Our immediate objective, first, is to release resources from home use, in order to reinforce the balance of trade, and to do this in a way which realises every practicable opportunity to reduce Government expenditure overseas. Second, it is to ensure that, as the economy moves into expansion, led by the priority areas I have mentioned – exports, import replacement, and investment – the total level of demand, public and private, is kept in line with what the productive machine can make available without lurching into inflation and excessive strain on our national resources.[7]

This quotation is notable for tying together the three most important macropolicy objectives of the time – external balance, growth of incomes and consumption, and prices stability – into a coherent statement about the general thrust of policy.

It would be misleading to suggest that resource planning was the sole preserve of successive Treasury White Papers. A separate initiative arose from attempts to plan the use of resources under the auspices of the Department of Economic Affairs. A useful example which reveals the kinds of pressures to curb spending which were prevalent then is given by Table 5.1. Shortly after that table appeared, and the DEA was abolished by the incoming

51

Conservative administration, the Treasury revised the data to reflect lower GDP growth prospects and indicate a greater commitment to private investment and consumption. This served to highlight the major perceived shortcoming of resource planning as it was practised in the 1960s: if the numbers could change radically as political administrations came and went then they would fail to retain credibility for very long.[8]

Events in the 1970s, while tending to discredit the Keynesian precepts upon which it was clearly based, nevertheless left the prior claims model intact as a planning tool.[9] The final flourish of the model came in 1976 with the PEWP of that year revealing a prior claims table with a variety of assumptions concerning GDP growth. This is reproduced here as Table 5.2. The table and supporting text suggest that, given the Labour administration of the time, personal consumption was by now regarded as the residual in the process of bids and claims. Whether in practice that

Table 5.1 *Possible use of resources 1967/72 (basic case)*

£ millions 1967 prices

	1967	Increase 1967/72
GDP at market prices	39093	6610
Balance of trade in goods and services [(1)]	−568	920
Investment		
Private industries and services	3056	890
Nationalised industries	1530	−40
Housing	1464	150
Public services	1033	480
Transfer cost of land and buildings	62	—
Stockbuilding	130	460
Defence[(2)]	2317	−380
Consumption		
Social and other public services	4746	1000
Personal	25323	3130

(1) Represents the demand on real resources. It is not the same as the balance of payments surplus.
(2) These figures cover current military defence expenditure on goods and services on the definitions used in the statistics of National Income and Expenditure published by the Central Statistical Office.
Source: Department of Economic Affairs, *The Task Ahead: Economic Assessment to 1972* (London: HMSO, 1969).

was so is rather doubtful. Although public expenditure was set at an invariant rate of 1 per cent growth, an even lower plan rate could have been inserted if the growth rate for personal consumption looked infeasibly low.[10]

Although the prior claims model is no longer referred to in public expenditure White Papers, an interesting prior claims projection for the 1980s may be reported. Davies and Piachaud[11] have put together such a projection using a central case of 2 per cent GDP growth.[12] Their tabulation depicts public expenditure as the residual after certain claims have been satisfied. These claims are:

- *Net Exports* returning to a level of about £1 billion per annum;
- *Investment*: rising to 14 per cent of GDP, as in 1979;
- *Consumers Expenditure*: assumed to grow in line with GDP in order to counteract wage pressures which would pose difficulties for the objective of prices stability.

This would allow growth of public consumption slightly in excess of GDP growth and contrasts with the objective of public expenditure stability proposed by the Government in 1984.[13] Their table is reproduced here as Table 5.3.

Finally, a fundamental problem with the resource planning model merits some discussion. It assumed a growth path for GDP and resource use over the medium term which was not necessarily consistent with actual economic policies being pursued in the short run. It might be supposed that the management of the economy requires:

- a set of consistent objectives for output, employment, inflation and the external sector;
- and a set of consistent, associated policy instruments targeted at those objectives.[14]

In practice, force of circumstance might often mean that budget decisions and exchange rate policies would be framed without consideration of the assumed GDP growth path in the resource planning framework.[15] However, it was possible to argue that this apparent inconsistency, should it arise, did not matter.

First, policy was concerned with the broad trend of resource availability and employment over a run of years, allowing a feasible assumption for public spending volume to be derived

53

Table 5.2 *The growth and use of resources 1974/79*   in demand terms at 1970 factor cost prices

| | Year 1974 | Average annual increase 1974–79 | | | | | |
| | | Case I | | Case II | | Case III | |
	£m.	£m.	%	£m.	%	£m.	%
A. SUPPLY OF RESOURCES							
1. Gross domestic product (GDP)	47200	1200	2.4	1720	3.4	1950	3.8
2. Net flow of resources into (+) or out of (−) balance of trade in goods and services	−200	500		560		600	
3. Available for domestic use (line 1 minus line 2)	47400	700	1.4	1160	2.3	1350	2.7
B. DOMESTIC USES OF RESOURCES							
1. Investment[1]							
a. Private investment	4700	350	6.5	490	8.7	550	9.6
b. Nationalised industries' investment	1300	50	4.0	50	4.0	50	4.0
2. Available for other public expenditure and private consumption (line A3 less lines B1a and B1b)	41400	300	0.7	620	1.4	750	1.7
C. USES OF RESOURCES FOR OTHER PUBLIC EXPENDITURE AND PRIVATE CONSUMPTION							
1. Public expenditure[2]							
a. Public consumption	9500	130	1.2	130	1.2	130	1.2
b. Other public investment	2300	−70	−3.5	−70	−3.5	−70	−3.5
c. Total direct public expenditure (a + b)	11800	60	0.5	60	0.5	60	0.5
d. Indirect public expenditure (transfers etc.)	6700	130	1.8	130	1.8	130	1.8
e. Total public expenditure (c + d)	18500	190	1.0	190	1.0	190	1.0
2. Personal consumption:							
a. Privately financed personal consumption (line B2 minus line C1e)	22900	110	0.5	430	1.8	560	2.3
b. Publicly financed personal consumption (indirect public expenditure, line C1d)	6700	130	1.8	130	1.8	130	1.8
c. Total personal consumption (C2a + C2b)	29600	240	0.8	560	1.8	690	2.2

Notes: (1) Private and nationalised industry investment comprise fixed investment and stockbuilding. Private investment excludes investment in housing, which is included in personal consumption.
(2) Excluding nationalised industry investment.
Source: 'Public Expenditure to 1979/80' (London: HMSO, February 1976) Cmnd. 6393, p. 6. For full footnotes see source.

Table 5.3 *Real resources available for public expenditure, 1983/88*

£bn 1980 prices

	1983 level	1988 illustrations assuming real GDP growth of:			Comments
		1% pa	2% pa	3% pa	
GDP (expenditure basis)	206.3	216.8	227.8	239.2	
Prior Claims:					
Net exports	2.7	1.1	1.1	1.1	Maintains current account balance in 1988
Private investment	27.9	30.3	31.9	33.5	Restores share in GDP to 1979 level
Stocks	0.7	0.7	0.7	0.7	Trend level maintained
Other Claims:					
Consumers expenditure	144.8	152.2	159.9	167.9	Grows in line with GDP
less factor cost adj.	32.0	33.6	35.3	37.1	Taxes and subsidies unchanged
Available for Public Exp:					
Total	62.2	66.1	69.5	73.1	
Public investment	11.7	12.7	13.4	14.1	Grows in line with private investment
Public consumption	50.5	53.4	56.1	59.0	
% growth pa 1983/88	—	1.2	2.2	3.3	

Source: G. Davies and D. Piachaud, 'Public Expenditure on the Social Services: The Economic and Political Constraints', in R. Klein and M. Higgins (eds) *The Future of Welfare* (Oxford: Basil Blackwell, 1985).

which would not be subject to disruptive and wasteful changes sought for short term policy reasons. This, it may be recalled, was an essential aim of the Plowden system. Second, the question had to be posed: are the policy instruments currently being employed in pursuit of short run economic objectives inconsistent, *on any conceivable scenario of economic developments*, with the economy achieving the assumed trend rate of GDP growth? An affirmative answer to that question was, and is, in the nature of things difficult to assert. An agnostic position was more likely; in which case it was not easy to be dogmatic about the inconsistency of the resource planning framework and the economic policies actually being pursued.

Indicative planning

A persistent shortcoming of the prior claims model in the context of demand management was that *direct* control could only be exercised over government consumption and investment. Government could attempt to influence the direction and degree of change in the remaining components of aggregate demand; but it had at best *indirect* control. However, the explicit tabulation of a resource planning framework aims to go beyond the use of indirect controls on private consumption, exports and investment. It had the further intention of indicating to the corporate sector a desired path for demand *and* output. 'Indicative planning', as it was labelled, thus had aspirations concerning the supply side of the economy. The government's reasons for embarking upon a system of indicative planning were never elaborated upon by official sources. However, economists have not been slow to fill the gap and an outline of the issues can be given here.[16]

Uncertainty exists in the market place and the environment. Entrepreneurs are uncertain about the prices and outputs which will be adopted by their competitors in the immediate and more distant future. They may over-estimate or under-estimate their aggression. Thus the aggregated production and marketing decisions of competitors in a market may exceed or fall short of the growth of demand in that market.

Entrepreneurs will also be uncertain about new discoveries, whether these are technological or natural resource discoveries. These two forms of uncertainty, *market* and *environmental* uncertainty, probably inhibit entrepreneurs from investing in their markets. Moreover, futures markets cannot be devised to eliminate the main sources of uncertainty.[17] Such a solution would be impossible because of the sheer number of futures markets required; and because, given that uncertainty about events twenty to thirty years ahead is at issue, some of the actors will be unable to participate.[18]

A *non-market* solution, which nevertheless stops short of 'normative' or central planning, is possible by employing indicative planning. By indicating a consensus growth path for aggregate demand and its components the planning agency could introduce orderliness and consistency into business plans. Individual entrepreneurs could be involved to a greater or lesser degree in the iterative discussions which eventually evolve into a credible growth path for the economy as a whole and its constituent parts. Such a process would tend to minimise shortages and surpluses in goods and factor markets, particularly labour markets.[19]

Indicative planning would thus hope to massage demand expectations positively such that a credible GDP growth path became a self-fulfilling target for all economic agents in the economy. As a study by the Political and Economic Planning group observed: 'The desirability of expansion has been alluded to from time to time but there has never been a clear aim expressed in terms that could enlist the enthusiasm of all sections of the community towards its fulfilment.'[20] There would also be spin-off benefits from the highlighting of critical shortages in factor markets and the co-ordination of individual investment plans over time.

In practice, as Budd has shown,[21] attempts at indicative planning during the 1960s foundered badly. Thus, while plan data gave the semblance of reduced uncertainty, in practice different expectations were held. The main sources of uncertainty could not be eliminated by multilateral discussions because industrialists would naturally incline towards aspirations or targets rather than realistic forecasts; or because under conditions of oligopolistic competition, where surprise is a powerful competitive tactic, industrialists were coy about their real intentions. Finally, many of the factors determining growth of demand were in fact exogenous to the UK and no matter how elaborate and technical the negotiations those factors could not be brought under control.

There were other drawbacks of indicative planning in practice[22] but for our purposes the main problem has been sketched. While the diagnosis of market shortcomings was admirable the non-market solution was found wanting. There was a fundamental inability to influence expectations because the numbers were simply not credible. Additionally, the experiment and subsequent failure with indicative planning would make future attempts to influence economic expectations that much more difficult to succeed. Yet this was precisely what government sought to do in the 1980s.

Summary

The prior claims model for assessing the prospects for public spending in Britain was based upon a standard Keynesian view of economic management. It aimed to fit the public sector's share of resources into an overall framework of competing sectoral claims. The view might be taken that the path for national output assumed in the model was never explicitly considered in framing actual demand management policies – hence, plans and economic policies were often inconsistent. Also, it may be argued that economic policies could never ensure any assumed path for output since the supply side of the economy was completely unresponsive to the variations in demand pressure applied. It may be supposed that it was for this reason that the planners borrowed ideas from the theory of indicative planning. However, failure to deliver the numbers in the plans helped to discredit this part of the machinery. Henceforth, economic expectations would be that much more difficult to influence.

6   The Advent of Cash Planning

The bare chronological facts leading to the adoption of cash planning have been narrated in Chapter 1. As the Treasury observed:

> For the first decade or more of the survey system, working in constant prices fitted well with what was then seen as the main role of macroeconomic policy – demand management. The emphasis in the public expenditure surveys was on planning 'real' resources for public expenditure within the framework of real resource projections for the economy as a whole. But it became increasingly apparent that the use of constant prices also has significant disadvantages for planning and control. These disadvantages have become greater in recent years with the higher and more variable rates of inflation and with the increasing emphasis of successive Governments on the control of monetary conditions. It is the actual 'cash spend' by Government which must be considered in relation to, and made consistent with, the Government's objectives for taxation, the borrowing requirement and the money supply.[1]

Cash planning was seen to have a number of advantages:

- in discussing the cash that has to be spent ministers would not be distracted by 'funny money' numbers in the PEWP;
- spending could be readily compared with revenue projections;
- cash costs could be brought into consideration – wage awards, for example, having clear cash consequences;
- cash spending could be translated directly into cash limits;
- rather than volume begetting finance, finance determined volume (departments would no longer regard a given volume provision as fixed regardless of what was happening to costs; this would help to sharpen up the search for efficiency gains to offset changes in cost).

Constant price planning was not without its advantages also; and a pro and con narrative may be constructed around the advent of cash planning. But radical change to the PES planning process did not simply arise from weighing up a balance of arguments about price bases.[2] Nor did it immediately follow the apparent loss of control over public spending in the mid-1970s (see Annex 1, Tables A.1 and A.2). Rather, a new planning philosophy was embraced dependent upon a revised view of the effectiveness of economic policy. This change in direction will be explored below. First, there will be an exposition of monetarist principles and the notion of 'rational expectations'. These are the theoretical concepts on which the new policy was based. The second task will be to describe the resultant structuring of economic policy. Those wishing to follow the argument fully will require elementary macroeconomics; others may skip the next two sections and pick up the story again in the section on policy implications.

Monetarism

At the heart of the monetarist analysis of money and prices is a smoothly functioning market mechanism. This Classical[3] assumption ensures that when there is excess supply (of goods or labour, for example) prices will tend to decline; and when there is excess demand prices will be bid upwards. In the Classical model such equilibrating forces are gradual but inevitable: they may take time to impose themselves, yet they will emerge, as surely as night follows day.

Thus, in the Classical analysis real wages equilibrate the supply of and demand for labour. The demand for labour, basically dependent on the marginal physical productivity of labour, will increase as the real wage (the nominal wage deflated by nominal prices) declines. On the other hand, if the real wage increases more labour will be willing to offer itself for financial reward. There will be one level of the real wage which will ensure that the quantity of labour supplied and labour demanded is equal. That is, price changes act to 'clear' the market of excess demand or supply. The same basic narrative holds for the goods market as for the labour market. The tendency for goods and labour markets to clear ensures that attempts to change employment and output will merely trigger off changes in nominal rather than real variables.

What will happen if, for example, there is a decline in the demand for consumer goods?

In the Classical model if there is a decline in the demand for goods, this creates an excess supply of goods and a tendency for prices to fall. A decline in prices with nominal wages unchanged results in an increasing real wage. An excess supply of labour will thus emerge, setting off a tendency for nominal wages to fall. In summary, both prices and nominal wages are tending to decrease. That is the equilibrating mechanism which eventually produces the original level of output in the goods market and employment in the labour market.

What are the predictions of the Classical model if public spending is expanded? An increase in public sector demand creates excess demand for goods and a tendency for goods prices to rise. This entails a fall in real wages. In turn, nominal wages will tend to rise as excess demand appears in the labour market. Thus price changes clear both markets.

How would Classical analysis handle an expansion in the money supply? Nominal money supply expansion creates excess demand for goods and goods prices rise. Rising goods prices with fixed nominal wages imply falling real wages and therefore an increasing demand for labour. Hence nominal wages also rise to preserve real wage equilibrium. Eventually these price and wage increases cause the real stock of money to decline towards its original level. In summary, then, a decline in the demand for consumer goods, or an increase in public sector demand, or an expansion of the money supply, have little impact on real variables, such as output and employment. The effect is at best transitory. There is a more lasting change in the nominal variables, the prices of goods and labour, which vary to ensure equilibrium in goods and labour markets.

The Classical system described above spells out the adjustment processes implicit in the standard textbook description of monetarist beliefs. This is based upon the Fisherian 'equation of exchange':

$$MV = PT$$

where:

- M is the nominal stock of money in circulation;
- V is the velocity of circulation of money (that is, the average

61

number of times the given quantity of money changes hands in transactions);

● P is the average price of transactions;
● T is the number of transactions that take place during the time period.

The 'equation' is an identity which must always be true. It states that the monetary value of spending in the economy must equal the monetary value of what is sold. For example, suppose that during a given time period, the number of transactions (T) is 1000 and that the average price of these transactions (P) is £5. Then it follows that the value of what is sold (PT) is £5000. If the money stock (M) is £500, then the average number of times each pound changes hands, the velocity of circulation (V), must be equal to 10.[4]

Monetarists take the view that T is not determined by money. It is affected by real variables acting on the goods and labour markets such as new resource discoveries, inventions, changes in the birth rate, and so on. T is therefore determined outside the system represented by the Fisherian equation of exchange. Also, V is held to be constant in the long run as institutional habits in employing money persist. With T as a given and V constant, M and P will be related; that is *causally* related as in the Classical system described above.

Modern reworkings of this theory admit V may vary in the short run (perhaps around as light but discernible trend), and allow an effect of M on T in the short run but not in the long run. Friedman's particular restatement elaborates the transmission mechanism from money to prices.[5] Friedman envisaged all wealth being held in a spectrum of assets which are more or less liquid. At one end of the spectrum is ready cash; at the other, physically immovable assets such as land. In between a variety of assets of declining liquidity – bank deposits, shares, antiques – are held. The whole portfolio is initially in a state of balance with each asset being held in a precisely desired proportion. An injection of cash entails a movement away from the desired balance; by moving out of money at the margin and into other assets balance can be reestablished. Such redistributions would obviously have consequences for the prices of non-cash assets.

Friedman's contribution was rather more than a sophisticated reconstruction of the Classical mechanism. But the economy was still seen as a system of interconnecting markets in each of which the assumption of flexible price clearing operated. The essential property of the system was, as stated at the outset of this section, a smoothly functioning market mechanism.

Rational expectations

A summary of what has been said above is: Classical analysis asserts that price and wage flexibility keep the economy at full employment output.[6] If the market mechanism does not work smoothly, if prices are sticky or even rigidly inflexible in practice, Classical analysis leaves something to be desired. With inflexible prices, a fall in demand can engender unemployment which persists for a long time; and an increase in demand will not be crowded out by price and interest rate increases. As explained in Chapter 5, this was the fundamental Keynesian insight. Keynes took the view that the market clearing mechanism works only very imperfectly. In contrast, an extreme monetarist or *new* Classical argument is that not only does the price mechanism work smoothly, it works instantaneously to keep an economy always very close to its full employment position.

New Classical thinking underpins wage and price flexibility with the notion of 'Rational Expectations'.[7] Rational expectations is shorthand for an assertion that people – wage earners, entrepreneurs, savers, consumers, investors, and so on – avoid systematic mistakes in forming expectations about the future. They take advantage of all the available data, use all the knowledge which they have accumulated about how the economy operates and make the best possible projections of the future. For these economic agents to be rational does not mean that henceforth they will not make forecasting errors. However, it does mean that they will not go on making the same mistakes in forming expectations time and time again. It would quickly dawn on them that they were consistently wrong and they would set about putting things right.

As well as forming expectations rationally economic agents take the view that the economy operates in the manner described by the Classical model. Thus, it will be *expected* that when, say, a fall in demand is observed goods prices are likely to fall, sooner or later.

Because goods prices are expected to fall, wage earners are quick to accept money wage cuts, correctly analysing that this implies no fall in real wages. Since money wage cuts are rapidly accepted actual goods prices can indeed be revised downwards. The more rapid the process whereby expectations are formed the more quickly the adjustment process can be completed and full employment maintained. In essence, 'thinking makes it so'.

A clear implication of the concept of rational expectations is what has been called 'instant monetarism' by Begg:

> A higher nominal money supply tends to boost aggregate demand. It will quickly lead to higher wages and prices to restore the real money supply to its former level. Interest rates are back to their old level and aggregate demand has returned to the full employment level.[8]

Thus, the concept of rational expectations may be seen as reinforcing belief in the Classical system.

Policy implications

The central message for policy-makers of the New Classicism is that output and employment cannot be moved away from their equilibrium or 'natural' level except in the very shortest of short runs. Any attempt to increase output and employment by means of fiscal or monetary policy will only lead to higher prices. The clear implication is that if there is to be an active macroeconomic policy it should be targeted at a variable which government policy can affect. Since government policy cannot affect real variables, output and employment, policy must be in respect of nominal variables – that is, the rate of inflation in prices. In so far as monetary growth determines inflation there should therefore be a policy of monetary control aimed at reducing inflation. Moreover, if expectations are rationally formed then policy should be consistent and predictable. If it is, economic agents will more readily perceive the inevitable consequences of those policy measures and act accordingly. Consistency breeds policy credibility and in consequence speeds up the process of expectations adjustment.

These ideas were very influential with policy-makers. As background to the Budget of 1980 the Treasury stated:

> Monetary policy is central to the Government's economic strategy. By maintaining strict control over the money stock, and ensuring that there is a progressive reduction in the rate of monetary growth in the years ahead, the Government intends to reduce substantially the rate of inflation and so help create the conditions necessary for sustained economic growth.[9]

The article went on to analyse post-war developments in money and prices in the context of the Fisherian equation of exchange; and use Friedmanite notions of portfolio balance to explain the transmission mechanism. The Treasury text also introduced the concept of the exchange rate transmission mechanism. Thus, restrictive monetary policies by reducing the demand for imports will put upward pressure on the exchange rate, directly reducing import prices. The less the authorities intervene in exchange markets the more rapidly will such tendencies emerge, reinforced in some measure by the sophisticated (rational) expectations of financial markets.[10]

It was thought that labour markets might be slow to adjust. With a higher exchange rate, lower imported goods prices and higher real wages, domestic goods prices and unit costs would be uncompetitive. If labour markets were slow to adjust markets would be lost and output and employment decline. It was imperative therefore to attempt to influence wage and salary earners' expectations: 'in order for expectations to adjust the Government must be seen to be serious about its targets for money supply. This is the rationale both for the Medium Term Financial Strategy and the importance the Government places on the credibility of its monetary targets.'[11]

The very sluggishness of expectations formation in labour markets would mean that a *gradualist* approach to economic policy was required. By announcing its unshakable intention to reduce inflation using monetary restraint government would eventually influence labour market expectations. The policy can thus be understood in the context of New Classical ideas although the monetary authorities stopped short of their complete endorsement.[12]

The medium term financial strategy (MTFS)

The MTFS was the systematic expression of the economic policies outlined above. The ideas of the system were clearly set out in the Mais Lecture by the Chancellor of the Exchequer in 1984.[13] There, macroeconomic policy was seen as addressing the problem of inflation, while microeconomic policies – including the liberalisation of goods and labour markets – attacked the problem of unemployment. In a highly stylised outline of the history of economic policy this could be characterised as a reversal of the conventional wisdom whereby macroeconomic policy, in particular fiscal policy, attempted to alleviate unemployment while microeconomic policies, such as incomes policy, sought to moderate inflationary pressures.

With inflation as the ultimate target of the system a path for the decline of inflation could be set into the future. It was plainly unrealistic to expect inflation of 10 to 15 per cent to be eliminated in a year or two, so that the medium term, a four or five year period, was targeted to achieve the virtual elimination of price inflation. This was thus the first target in a hierarchy of ultimate and intermediate targets.

Second, a credible rate for the growth of Gross Domestic Product was projected, largely dependent on growth in the supply of factors of production, and productivity from those factors. Together with the path for prices this prediction therefore set a path for money GDP. In terms of the Fisherian equation of exchange the right-hand-side expression for PT was thus 'given' as an assumption. Third, an assumption about velocity of circulation was required. Largely informed by trend considerations this would clearly be highly conjectural.[14] Nevertheless, once a feasible range of velocity assumptions had been decided upon then a range for the growth of the monetary aggregates would be implied (dividing both sides of the Fisherian equation of exchange by V):

$$M = \frac{PT}{V}$$

Next, the strategy needed a set of policy instruments to deliver M. In theory, control of the money aggregates could be established solely by means of changes in interest rates. However, the monetary authorities would not wish to allow interest rates to do all the work of control. At times that would mean unacceptably high and volatile interest rates. Thus: '... the money stock can be controlled by an appropriate combination of fiscal policy and interest rates; supported as necessary by operations in gilt-edged markets'.[15]

It will help to clarify what is at issue here by digressing briefly on monetary accounting identities. A simplified expression for the increase in the money supply is:

	1	2	3	4
increase in the money stock	= public sector borrowing requirement	sales of public sector debt to non-bank private sector	+ increase in bank lending to the private sector	+ net external flows

The first item on the right hand side of this relationship is the Public Sector Borrowing Requirement (PSBR), which is the financial deficit of the public sector plus a few national accounts adjustments.[16] To some extent this deficit may be financed by the second item, which consists of sales of gilt edge securities to non-bank holders. The third item is the private sector lending activities of banks, for houses, cars, business finance, and so on. The fourth item, usually much the smallest of those on the right hand side, is simply the net result of similar transactions to the first three, but which involve an overseas resident.

Concentrating on the first three components – known as 'Domestic Credit Expansion' – it can readily be seen that to restrain the increase in the money stock requires restraint of public and private demand for money, or offsetting sales of gilt edge stocks to the public. If the public sector deficit is not subject to a limit then control can be exercised by ruthlessly restraining private demand and selling large amounts of gilts. However, in both those cases the consequences could be unacceptably high and volatile interest rates.[17]

The pragmatic expression of all these considerations was the system of intermediate and ultimate targets known as the Medium Term Financial Strategy, set out in successive Financial Statement and Budget Reports. Table 6.1 depicts the MTFS targets up to

1985. The ultimate target, the rate of inflation in the price of goods, was not precisely specified. However, actual inflation rates have been inserted at the foot of the table. The figures largely speak for themselves. As the years have gone by the early lack of success in hitting targets has been improved upon; price inflation is now hovering in the single digit range. The list of intermediate targets was augmented in 1986 but the general thrust of the strategy – with a PSBR target and control ranges for the monetary aggregates – remained the same.[18] It is, of course, entirely possible that the progressively improved picture on inflation is unrelated to hitting the MTFS targets and that the measure of success with price inflation has been achieved by trading-off against employment and favourable commodity price developments.[19]

The set of PSBR targets in the MTFS directly implied cash planning of public expenditure. Thus, on the receipts side of the public sector financial account were taxes, national insurance contributions, local authority rates, and so on, *and* a borrowing target. The cash sum of public expenditure was constrained to equal the sum of those receipt items. In this sense, public expenditure was the cash residual of the MTFS. Moreover, it would be an administrative nonsense to maintain a survey price system of public spending control as well as the MTFS-derived cash plan for such spending. That would have created intolerable difficulties for those having to construct the 'read-across' from one to the other. Thus it was no surprise that, in the event, survey price planning was abolished.

The above outline neglects any actual iterations preceding the final figures in the MTFS. In practice if the aspiration for a particularly low PSBR suggests an implausibly low cash planning total, the Treasury looks again at the whole set of public sector accounts, including the MTFS intermediate targets, and reworks the data. The narrative here is to a certain extent stylised and does not aim to do full justice to the complexity of the strategy as a whole.

Summary

Although on a departmental basis spending plans are conceived primarily in volume terms, that is, in terms of what money will

Table 6.1 *The Medium Term Financial Strategy: projections and outturns*

	1979/80	1980/81	1981/82	1982/83	1983/84	1984/85	1985/86	1986/87	1987/88	1988/89
Money supply: £M3 (per cent change)										
June 1979[1]	9	—	—	—	—	—	—	—	—	—
March 1980	—	7–11	6–10	5–9	4–8	—	—	—	—	—
March 1981	—	—	6–10	5–9	4–8	—	—	—	—	—
March 1982	—	—	—	8–12	7–11	6–10	—	—	—	—
March 1983	—	—	—	—	7–11	6–10	5–9	—	—	—
March 1984	—	—	—	—	—	6–10	5–9	4–8	3–7	2–6
March 1985	—	—	—	—	—	—	5–9[2]	4–8	3–7	2–6
Actual[3]	16.2	19.4	12.8	11.2	9.4	11.9	16.9	—		
Public sector borrowing requirement (%GDP)										
June 1979	4.5									
March 1980	—	3.75	3	2.25	1.5	—	—	—	—	—
March 1981	—	—	4.25	3.25	2	—	—	—	—	—
March 1982	—	—	—	3.5	2.75	2	—	—	—	—
March 1983	—	—	—	—	2.75	2.5	2	—	—	—
March 1984	—	—	—	—	—	2.25	2	2	1.75	1.75
March 1985	—	—	—	—	—	—	2	2	1.75	1.75
Actual (%)	4.8	5.6	3.4	3.2	3.2	3.1	1.6	—		
Actual (£b)	10.0	12.7	8.6	8.9	9.7	10.2	5.8			
Inflation (RPI All Items %	15.8	16.3	11.5	7.1	4.7	5.1	5.9	3.2	—	—

1. A target for the ten months to April 1980 appeared in the June 1979 Budget.
2. The 5 to 9 per cent target for the growth of sterling M3 in 1985/86 was abandoned on 17 October 1985.
3. Seasonally adjusted annualised rates for relevant periods.

Sources: *Financial Statement and Budget Report*, various years; *Financial Statistics*.

buy, public sector expenditure is now first and foremost the subject of a medium term cash plan.

Thinking in cash terms naturally grew from a conviction that macroeconomic policy was powerless to influence the stability of output and employment. This conviction grew from the belief that neo-Keynesian policies had outlived their usefulness and that an efficiently working market mechanism tends to neutralise policy attempts to actively manage demand. Such neutralisation would mean that policies aimed at raising money GDP would engender price changes rather than output and employment changes.

The Medium Term Financial Strategy was based upon these precepts. Because macroeconomic policies were believed to impact primarily on prices they had an inflation target as the ultimate objective. In a monetarist perspective that implied the articulation of monetary aggregate targets. If the control of the monetary aggregates was managed by one instrument, namely interest rates, it would entail excessive interest rate variability and, at times, unacceptably high interest rates. Therefore, control of the PSBR in quantitative terms was sought as a complement to interest rate control. Targets for the PSBR were thus incorporated into the MTFS. Given a cash target for borrowing, and assuming a certain level of tax receipts, public spending could be derived as a cash residual of the MTFS.

7 A Perspective on Cash Planning

Cash planning was introduced in 1981 to take effect in the financial year 1982/83. The intention was to operate in 3-year cycles with a medium term cash plan. Therefore, an analysis of the cash outturns for the first two cash planning cycles is possible. Alternatively, the objectives of the MTFS may be viewed in the light of outturns for public spending, borrowing and taxes in relation to GDP. As was noted in Chapters 3 and 6, these GDP-based data have assumed some importance as intermediate, and perhaps ultimate, targets of the strategy. Thus there are three objectives: to establish how successful has been the aim of sticking to cash plans; to gain an impression of the volume consequences of cash planning; and to assess the pattern of GDP-based outturns for spending, borrowing and taxation.

Cash plans versus cash outturns

The first of these tasks is relatively straightforward. The Treasury now publishes in the annual White Paper on expenditure plans a useful table describing cash plans and outturns on a constant definition basis.[1] The relevant portions are reproduced here as Table 7.1. From this it can readily be seen that in the first cash planning cycle over 1981/2 to 1984/5 a planned growth of £22 billions was envisaged, or just under 21 per cent. In the event, the cash plan was exceeded by just over £2 billions. In the second complete cycle, that stretching over 1982/3 to 1985/6 a cash growth of over £19 billions was planned. In this case the outturn exceeded plans by about £1¼ billions.

However, those figures do not give the complete picture. The constant definition table does not take account of the abolition of

Table 7.1 *Public expenditure plans and outturns*

£billion

	1981/2	1982/3	1983/4	1984/5	1985/6	1986/7	1987/8	1988/9
March 1982 White Paper (Cmnd. 8494)	105.7	114.7	120.7	127.7				
Feb 1983 White Paper (Cmnd. 8789)	104.6	113.1	119.6	126.5	132.3			
Feb 1984 White Paper (Cmnd. 9143)	104.6	113.4	120.4	126.5	132.1	136.8		
Jan 1985 White Paper (Cmnd. 9428)	104.6	113.5	120.3	128.2	132.1	136.8	141.6	
Jan 1986 White Paper Cmnd. 9702)	103.9	113.4	120.3	129.6	134.2	139.1	143.9	
Jan 1987 White Paper (Cmnd. 56)	104.0	113.5	120.3	129.8	133.6	140.4	148.6	154.2

Note: Figures to the left of the stepped outline are outturns or estimated outturns. Figures to the right of the stepped outline are plans.

Source: HM Treasury, *The Government's Expenditure Plans 1987/88 to 1989/90* (London: HMSO, Cmnd. 56–I) Table 1.9, p. 19.

the National Insurance Surcharge (NIS) during the first cash plan cycle. This surcharge stood at 3½ per cent of earnings in April 1982. It was quickly dismantled for employers in the private sector, and progressively abolished for public sector exployers over 1982/4.[2] The Chancellor noted that the abolition of the surcharge was not intended to make room for extra spending by the public sector agencies affected; the sums involved would be clawed back.[3] Thus, the data in Table 7.1 have to be adjusted for the amounts in the original plans which, because of NIS abolition, overstated requirements.

However, an adjustment for this factor poses a problem. Successive Autumn Statements in 1982 and 1983 give some idea of the sums involved (in the section dealing with illustrative tax changes) but the decision to opt for gradual abolition in the public sector made the picture unclear. No authoritative estimate by Government has ever been published of the total impact had NIS abolition taken effect in one year.[4] Data in a table produced by Ward[5] indicate that the effect may be of the order of £1½ to £2 billions in 1984/5 prices. If this rough estimate is usable the cash slippage on the first two cash planning cycles is approximately £3 to £4 billions, or between 2 to 3 per cent of the target.

The tentative nature of the figuring must be stressed. Moreover, the temptation to treat the first plan figure as a tablet of stone must be resisted. There *are* changes of policy and irresistible events even in an avowedly cash planning world. There are also some spending areas, especially in the local authority sphere, where it would be unwise to imagine that central government has more than nominal control. Nevertheless, the general upward drift of the cash figures – which appears to have continued into the third cash planning cycle – is unmistakeable.

Cash and real spending

Cash planning must be seen in the context of the MTFS, as Chapter 6 sought to show. Hence the assessment of the cash planning régime has to be primarily in terms of whether or not the cash targets were stuck to. However, the volume implications of cash planning cannot be ignored entirely. Although volume is a secondary consideration, under cash planning the government is still willing to take a view on the desirable path of real public spending. Moreover, it is difficult to believe that departmental officials are not concerned with real spending trends as plans have to be based on assumptions about what money will buy, that is, volume.[6] Thus, it is instructive to contrast cash allocations with spending data in real terms.

The concept of real terms spending pursued in the public expenditure White Paper is total cash spending adjusted by a GDP price deflator. The GDP deflator is a domestic economy price deflator which is useful for measuring the opportunity cost of public spending in terms of final goods and services. It cannot be used to guage the real volume of inputs in the public sector.[7] This is because there are sound reasons for supposing that the price deflator appropriate to public sector inputs differs systematically from the GDP deflator. Why that should be so is taken up below. For the moment, the Government data on real terms spending are displayed in Table 7.2. It is important to realise that these are overall figures and that individual departments may have spending histories very different from the average.

The global picture is one of steady annual increases in volume until 1985/86 when spending was reined back. Volume growth was resumed in 1986/87. These results are confirmed by the departmental spending data (gross of central privatisation proceeds) in the first row of the table.[8] There appears to be input volume growth of 6 per cent from the base year of 1981/82 up to 1986/87, a period during which it was the intention of Government to keep public spending broadly stable in real terms.[9] Departmental

Table 7.2 *The planning total in PEWP real terms, 1981–82 to 1986–87*

	1981/2	1982/3	1983/4	1984/5	1985/6	1986/7
				£millions, 1984/85 prices		
Department spending	129404	131621	134256	139823	136324	141100
Central privatisation proceeds	−611	−564	−1262	−2260	−2702	−4619
Planning Total	128793	131057	132994	137563	133622	136500
Percent change on previous year	—	+1.8	+1.5	+3.4	−2.9	+2.2

The figure for the 1986/7 PEPT is the estimated outturn and has been rounded to reflect its provisional nature.

Source: H M Treasury, *1987 PEWP*, Cmnd. 56–II, Table 2.2, p. 8.

spending advanced by some 9 per cent over the same period. Some (about £2½ billions), but not all of this growth may be attributed to special factors in 1984/85. However, the appeal to special factors carries little conviction for the comparison of 1986/87 with 1981/82, when all of the effect of the coal strike had been unwound.

The above discussion is predicated on the assumption that the data in Table 7.2 are a meaningful series for real terms spending. It is now time to relax that assumption and to examine the usefulness of the GDP deflator in analysing public spending trends.

The relative price effect

The relative price effect is the tendency whereby the prices paid for public sector inputs systematically differ from private sector prices. It may be illustrated by reference to a two sector model of the domestic economy. Thus we imagine that the domestic economy is composed of two sectors, private and public. In time period 1 the following data are given:

		Public Sector	Private Sector
1.	Inputs	100	100
2.	Outputs	100	100
3.	Value of outputs	100	100
4.	Price of outputs ($^3/_2$)	1.0	1.0

In time period 2, both sectors are affected by inflation in earnings which is passed on in output prices:

		Public Sector	Private Sector
1.	Inputs	100	100
2.	Outputs	100	101.5
3.	Value of outputs	105	105
4.	Prices of outputs ($^3/_2$)	1.05	1.035

However, the private sector is able to obtain a productivity improvement of about 1½ per cent and is thus able to pass on a per unit price increase rather less than that passed on by the public sector. Hence, public sector prices increase relative to those in the private sector.

75

The public sector will be unable to partly offset the increased cost of inputs in the same way because it cannot register productivity improvements. The reason why such productivity improvements do not appear is that, by national accounting convention, the *output* of the public sector is not separately measured: any changes in output are a direct one-to-one consequence of changes in *inputs*. Hence productivity changes, decrements as well as increments, are ruled out by definition. It does not matter that in government productivity improvements may be difficult or easy to obtain; or that the measurement of such changes poses considerable conceptual difficulties; for the purposes of accounting for activity in the national economy such gains are ignored.

In the stylised illustration given above it would have been possible to obtain the same change in the price of output for the public sector as for the private sector by holding down public sector input costs (and, therefore, the value of outputs). For example, a stringent incomes policy could have been assumed. As Price has observed, this strategy has been attempted by successive administrations, without success in the longrun.[10] Earnings in the two sectors tend to grow together in the medium to long run whatever short term success incomes policies enjoy. The actual size of the relative price effect in the UK was of the order illustrated in the model, plus 1½ per cent, over the period 1962 to 1979.[11] However, that 1½ per cent is an average for the whole public sector over the long run. In any one year the relative price effect may be smaller than 1½ per cent, or even negative. For individual departments also, the relative price effect need bear little relation to the average.

Some notion of the overall size of the relative price effect in recent years may be gleaned from Table 7.3. The GDP deflator and the retail prices index require no further explanation. The General Government Final Consumption (GGFC) deflator is based on estimates of final consumption on goods and services by central and local government. It thus excludes most financial transfer spending including subsidies, grants, and national insurance benefits. The GGFC index is an *implied* index; that is, it is constructed by dividing cash sums spent by a 'constant price' estimate of GGFC. As indicated in the stylised model discussed above changes in this estimate of constant price GGFC depend largely on input information – numbers of employees weighted by grade, for example – although there is a substantial component of bought-in goods and services for which there are specific price indices used to deflate cash sums spent.[12]

Table 7.3 *A comparison between deflators*

	(1) Annual change in GDP deflator %	(2) Annual change in general government final consumption deflator %	(3) Annual change in retail prices index %
1981/82	8.21	15.60	11.49
1982/83	7.23	8.39	7.08
1983/84	5.16	4.95	4.66
1984/85	4.75	5.86	5.06
1985/86	5.59	5.53	5.93

Source: CSO, *National Income and Expenditure*, and *Economic Trends*.

In the comparison between the first two deflators, apart from the abnormal year of 1981/82,[13] the relative price effect is twice positive and twice just negative, suggesting that recent experience is atypical. The reasons why the recent past has departed from the sort of narrative common in the 1960s and 1970s may be speculated upon. Increased competition in certain industries has allowed government agencies to obtain highly competitive price quotations – this factor is thought to have operated in the transport construction sector, for example.[14] But the major reason for the departure from the norm may be cash planning itself, which attempts to put a fixed limit on the numerator used in the construction of the GGFC deflator. Given the number of special factors affecting such public sector price indices there is little prospect of obtaining a credible real terms series for input volume. Robinson has attempted to do so for the welfare spending departments, using a variety of lesser-known sources.[15] However, no aggregate series has been constructed by an official body.

Table 7.4 uses the GGFC deflator and the RPI deflator from Table 7.3 to construct a real terms input series from the cash planning totals in Table 7.1. This shows that after the coal strike year of 1984/85 there was a considerable fall in volume. Nevertheless, over the whole period of cash planning there has been a volume increase of about 2 per cent. Thus, in real terms public spending was not kept broadly stable, as the Government hoped. However, the limitations of the data must be remembered when interpreting this finding.

Table 7.4 *The planning total in real terms*

	(1) Cash planning total £ millions	(2) Real terms planning total* 1985/86 basis	(3) Per annum change in (2) %
1981/82	103 987	131 072	—
1982/83	113 469	132 648	+1.20
1983/84	120 319	134 185	+1.16
1984/85	129 777	137 183	+2.23
1985/86	133 622	133 622	−2.60

Note: The GGFC and RPI deflators in Table 7.3 have been current-weighted using the proportion of public spending in purchases of goods and services, other public sector pay and departmental running costs as the GGFC weight; and the proportion of public spending in personal, corporate and overseas transfers as the RPI weight. Thus the GGFC deflator has been applied to those parts of public spending which are in fact final consumption; but for transfers an index more accurately reflecting the spending power remitted to final consumers is employed.

Source: HM Treasury, *PEWP 1987*, Cmnd. 56–II, Table 2.7; for the deflators the sources noted in Table 7.3.

GDP-Related Objectives

The 1984 Green Paper on tax burdens in the medium term set out an integrated structure of objectives for public spending, borrowing and taxes as a proportion of GDP.[16] More recently, the expenditure White Papers have laid emphasis on the relationship between general government expenditure and GDP. Indeed, the 1987 PEWP contains a table showing plans and outturns with respect to this ratio.[17]

General government expenditure[18] is financed by taxes, national insurance contributions, interest and dividends, a variety of other receipts, and borrowing. So there is not a precise equation between spending on the one hand and taxes and borrowing on the other. Nevertheless, given that taxes currently finance about 70 per cent of general government expenditure (GGE), and that government has targets for GGE/GDP, it is possible to infer a related target for taxes as a percentage of GDP. The 1984 Green Paper certainly implied the existence of a medium term objective to reduce the taxation burden in relation to GDP; and the 1986 FSBR stated: 'The measures in the Budget are designed to strengthen these policies [the MTFS and microeconomic policies] and to reduce the burden of taxation and the role of the state in the economy. Both tax and expenditure are on a declining path as a proportion of Gross Domestic Product'[19]

Finally, the status of PSBR/GDP targets in the MTFS was discussed in Chapter 6 above. It is interesting to observe, as in Table 7.5, that the general experience with this loose structure of targets is one of relative failure up to 1984/85; and modest success since then. It remains to be seen whether improvements in these intermediate performance indicators will be directly related to changes in prices, output and employment.

Table 7.5 *A constellation of GDP-related objectives*

	Prev Year's Planned GGE/GDP	Actual GGE/GDP	Prev Year's Planned PSBR/GDP	Actual PSBR/GDP	Tax as per cent GDP
1983/84	—	45¾	2¾	3¼	31
1984/85	44½	45¾	2¼	3	31½
1985/86	45	44	2	1½	31¼

Notes: Figures are rounded to the nearest quarter per cent. GGE: General Government Expenditure: See Annex 1.
Taxes are taxes on income, expenditure and capital as in *Financial Statistics*, Tables 2.1 and 2.2
GDP is at current market prices.
Sources: *PEWP* 1987, Cmnd. 56–I; *FSBR* 1984, 1985, 1986; *Financial Statistics*

Summary

The cash planning régime may be assessed in terms of the ability to stick to cash targets – the intermediate objective of the MTFS system. Some success has been achieved here although cash slippages of between £3 and £4 billions over the first three cash planning cycles may have given cause for concern.

The input volume consequences of cash planning are not easily perceived, largely owing to the absence of suitable statistical information on public sector prices. The somewhat defective data to hand indicate that there has been an unplanned increase in volume during the period of cash planning. However, the increase was just under 2 per cent and confidence in the data is such that this unofficial version of the true statistical picture must be used with caution.

Finally, it is possible to treat the objectives for spending, taxation and borrowing (all related to GDP) as the performance indicators arising out of the MTFS and cash planning. Seen in this light alone, the data suggest a modest improvement in the government's overall performance.

In Conclusion: The Future

The PES process is in a more or less permanent disequilibrium state. It would be naive to expect the system now established to stand still; nothing in the economic environment positively suggests that change will henceforth abruptly cease. Pressure for change arises from a number of sources. Spending priorities change, and clearly impinge upon a resource bidding system; political pressure for the implementation of greater or lesser financial control may emerge; external events, including comparisons with systems elsewhere, can engender change; gratified surprise at what can be achieved with one initiative for change can itself give rise to further thrusts for reform.

There are three ways in which the process of planning public spending may develop in the medium term:

- towards a more explicitly rational ordering of priorities within and between departments;
- introducing real terms comparisons over time which allow for the relative price effect;
- integrating PES documentation with the Estimates system.

The first two of these developments are related to the growing information base held in departments as a result of the Financial Management Initiative; the third development has a compelling logic which PES planners already recognise.

The PES and the Financial Management Initiative

As we have seen, the PES is less obviously a resource allocation process than the ritualised preamble to a set of fairly successful spending control procedures. The Survey cannot pretend to have

81

much appeal as a sophisticated rationing mechanism even if it performs reasonably well as the servant of macroeconomic control. However, the PES may yet mature to provide an explicitly rational basis for spending priorities, both within *and* between departments. Such a development would certainly be welcomed by the Treasury and Civil Service Committee, which has consistently enquired about the intellectual basis of spending decisions, and has expressed sincere doubts as to whether cross-departmental trade-offs are ever considered in Cabinet.

The Treasury is not insensitive to such criticism. Part of its answer is that the search for 'value for money' is an integral component of the survey process:

> Value for money from public expenditure is as important as the planning and monitoring of the total spent on programmes. The test for the Government, Parliament and the taxpayer has to be what is being bought or achieved with the money. So a constant theme running through the public expenditure process is better planning and management to increase value for money year by year. That means starting with a clear view of what could be achieved, *deciding the priority objectives*, and then pursuing them in the most efficient way.[1]

Thus the PES process must start with an ordering of priorities. This point was amplified by the Chief Secretary to the Treasury in a presentation to the Public Finance Foundation in July 1986.[2] He suggested there that value for money cannot be pursued as an overriding aim without explicit consideration of priorities.

Much of the information on efficiency and effectiveness which can be employed to establish priorities is emerging from the Financial Management Initiative (FMI) systems operated by departments (see Chapter 2).[3] These are primarily a tool for performance review and improved cash control by top management. Published accounts of these systems show that they cover aims, objectives, resources, output targets and performance against targets for the immediate past and, in some cases, for forthcoming periods.[4] The uses of FMI systems are seen as threefold by the central departments encouraging their development:

- meeting the needs of ministers and senior managers to decide strategic priorities and allocate resources within departments;
- managing programmes with closer control over objectives, better measures of cost and performance, and more sophisticated appraisal systems;
- developing budgetary control systems.[5]

FMI systems thus seek to allocate, manage and control using a basis of management accounting data on inputs *and* outputs.

While these systems may provide adequate information upon which to assess priorities within departments, there is a vacuum where inter-departmental priorities are concerned (see Chapter 4). That is an imbalance which can only get more obvious with the passing of time. Hence this is one area where the data arising from departmental FMI systems could be adapted and augmented to permit comparisons between the major spending programmes. That requires departmental FMI systems to become more comparable in terms of measures of inputs and outputs. Inevitably this requires that departments will have to espouse standard cost effectiveness analysis, cost-benefit analysis, and implied value analysis techniques. There is some evidence from the annual public expenditure White Papers and elsewhere that this is occurring, if rather slowly. Much probably remains to be achieved.

One area where FMI developments are already having an impact on the PES is in running costs control.[6] Without the budgetary control systems which have been developed in departments during the past few years it is doubtful whether running cost limits, as distinct from overall cash limits, would be feasible. As a Treasury spokesperson has observed:

> The concept of running costs – which is to give departments a provision within which they can work and adjust their items of expenditure as matters change during the year – fits with the grain of the delegated responsibility for budgeting and for management which is part of the Financial Management Initiative – developments which are going on in departments for improving line management's responsibility and accountability for expenditure under its control.[7]

The implementation of running costs control is a useful advance. But, once more, it is an advance in terms of financial control. It may be some time before progress can be reported upon the use of FMI systems to inform the allocation of resources between departments.

PES and Real Terms

PES money is cash. Cash has all but driven out real terms expressions of spending from the annual White Paper.

The emphasis on cash in current official expenditure presentations has many appeals. *Planning in cash* to obtain *value for money* appears, more than just superficially, to be a logical coupling. The current system also has undoubted presentational advantages over the old survey price system for non-experts accustomed to thinking and planning in cash terms. It is worth recalling, too, that the ultimate aim of the MTFS is virtual non-inflation of prices and in a continuously non-inflationary world, cash and constant price systems would be indistinguishable.

Until the official target of zero inflation is reached, however, there is a case for introducing realistic deflators to give departments and Parliament some notion of how inputs and, where appropriate monetary measures are possible, outputs are changing. Input and output targetry does not make full sense unless all the targets are in volume terms or, what comes to the same thing, in cash deflated to a real terms series. Cross-departmental comparisons of targets ought to be possible if the latter route is chosen.

Consider the following list of targets put forward as examples of good practice in targetry by the Chief Secretary to the Treasury:

● by improved targeting, which involved directing the available resources further away from a uniform visiting pattern towards the areas of greater revenue risk, Customs and Excise have met their target to increase the tax recovered by VAT control visits by 7 per cent;

● regional health authorities cost improvement programme which has a target to find £150 million new cash-releasing improvements this year;

● DES targets for removing surplus school places: 1 125 000 by 1987 with further targets for later years.[8]

84

All of these targets could have been expressed in cash and, in turn, cash could have been deflated to a common basis in order to compare and contrast the ambition of departments. A further basis for comparison would have been made possible by expressing such real terms targets in relation to the departmental spending required to achieve the targets.

The current practice, as the main text has shown (see Chapter 7), is to portray cash spending, at a high level of aggregation of departmental spend, deflated by the GDP deflator. While this helps to see public spending in an economy-wide, opportunity cost framework[9] the resulting series shows the effect of input volume increases, and the effect of relative price increases in the public sector, conflated together. The Treasury has argued that this is a *benefit* of using the GDP deflator.[10]

It remains to be seen whether a change of view will eventually emerge. The information which is held in departments would undoubtedly allow real terms comparisons, as Robinson has shown.[11] However, some tangible benefits from the reintroduction of departmental deflators, such as an improved basis for the comparison of performance targets – and even interdepartmental priorities – may be required to change attitudes.

Integration with estimates

The Estimates system starts into action late in the calendar year with cash requests made to Parliament in the spring and summer of the following year.[12] Not all of the cash requirements flowing from public spending decisions are voted by Parliament, as has been explained in the main text (see Chapter 3). Nevertheless, a considerable proportion is. The other sources of finance for spending decisions – in the main, the National Insurance fund, and rent and rates raised by local authorities – do not involve Parliamentary sanction.

Thus, there is a patchwork of sources of funds. It would make the public expenditure White Paper a much more useful document if the means of financing programmes were seen to follow on from the main spending proposals. At present the annual White Paper and the Supply Estimates volumes are linked together by a Summary and Guide.[13] The latest of these for 1986 shows that some thought has clearly been given to making the read-across from the PEWP to Estimates simpler.[14] But such simplifications merely serve to highlight the oddity of a system which keeps spending proposals separate from financing instruments. Private individuals and corporations could not survive for long with such an artificial divorce between spending plans and their funding. If there were to be a more comprehensive PEWP with added funding detail such a development would be the least surprising of the three main developments pointed to in this postscript.

Annex 1   The Definition of Public Expenditure[1]

The domestic economy may be depicted thus:

Central Government ⎫ General   ⎫ Public ⎫
Local authorities   ⎬ Government ⎬ Sector ⎬
Public Corporations ⎭   ⎭   ⎪
                                            ⎬ Domestic
Industrial and Commercial Companies ⎫ Private ⎫ Economy
Financial Companies and Institutions ⎬ Sector ⎬
Personal Sector   ⎭   ⎭

Up to 1977 the definition of public expenditure was based on measures of *public sector* activity. After that date the focus progressively narrowed until 1987 when accounts of public spending related almost exclusively to the *General Government* sector. In order to preserve continuity the term 'public expenditure' is still used.

Thus, up until 1977, public expenditure was treated as consisting of:

(i)   the current and capital expenditure of central and local government;
(ii)   the capital expenditure of public corporations;
(iii) gross debt interest paid by general government and the public corporations to other sectors.

In 1977 the capital expenditure of virtually all public corporations was excluded from the definition. However, government finance to public corporations in the form of grants and loans was retained. A further change was introduced in 1978: all the external and foreign market borrowing of public corporations, hitherto regarded as receipt items, was included in the control total of public expenditure. The reason for this was the increased emphasis placed on control of money market conditions by the Labour administration of the time.[2]

For 1977 and 1978 *net* debt interest replaced gross debt interest as it represented the actual financing commitment. Then in 1979 debt interest was dropped from the newly-coined expression of *public expenditure planning total*. Nevertheless, debt interest, in gross terms, is still included when comparing public expenditure with Gross Domestic Product. The rationale for excluding debt interest from the planning total is:

● debt interest cannot be planned in any meaningful sense in that the National Debt is largely inherited and the interest rates on that inherited debt are not wholly controlled by the Government;
● there would be an element of double-counting because spending allocations to local authorities include amounts used to pay interest.

Thus in 1987 the public expenditure planning total (PEPT) consisted of:

● current and capital (positive and negative[3]) spending of general government;
● capital spending of some small public corporations;
● government grants and loans and external finance of the remaining public corporations;
● an unallocated reserve.

This definition was thought to be reasonably close to standard international practice – sufficiently close to make comparisons between the UK and other countries worthwhile.

Up until the 1986 White Paper a concept of Public Expenditure (PE), was used in a ratio relation with GDP. To derive PE three additions were made to the PEPT:

● Public Sector (that is, general government and public corporations) *net* debt interest;
● The capital consumption of non-trading government services;
● VAT paid by local authorities but repaid to them.

However, in the 1987 White Paper the PE concept was dropped and a concept of General Government Expenditure (GGE) employed. This used *Gross General Government* debt interest

88

rather than *Net Public Sector* debt interest; and some minor national accounts adjustments are also made. The main distinction between PE and GGE is, therefore, that PE includes only the net financing commitment to be borne by taxes, borrowing, rates, etc; whereas GGE measures gross financial flows.

The following tables from Stibbard's excellent article give a comprehensive picture of the main magnitudes discussed above. While cash figures for the PEPT (Column 4, Table A.1) almost trebled in the first decade, in the subsequent decade the cash PEPT more than quadrupled. In what are described as real terms by Stibbard (that is, the GDP deflator is used rather than a deflator specific to the public sector) there was over 62 per cent growth in the first decade and only 16 per cent growth in the second decade.

One ratio not given great prominence in discussion of public spending is shown in Table A.4. This is the ratio of public spending on goods and services as a proportion of GDP (Column 5). With this ratio the components appearing in the numerator also appear in the denominator; a like-with-like measure of GDP resource use and absorption is therefore made possible. The ratio has remained broadly stable since the early 1970s. The more familiar GGE/GDP ratio, also in Table A.4 (Column 2), includes financial transfers in the numerator. However, transfers of claims on resources, as opposed to actual resources, cannot appear in the GDP denominator. Neither can sales of capital assets (which are included in the PEPT, PE, and GGE definitions of the numerator) because the act of changing the ownership of existing assets does not directly generate national income. Thus, it is not clear what changes in this ratio indicate.

Table A.5 describes the links between the three main definitions of public spending. Finally, Table A.6 is a very useful portrayal of how public spending is financed. If the annual public expenditure White Paper were to develop in the direction presaged in the concluding chapter of the text this table would provide a useful summary of sources of funds.

Table A.1 *Measures of public spending (in cash)*

	Pre-1977 public expenditure definition	General government expenditure	1985 planning total definition	1985 planning total excluding PCMOB[1]
1963/64	111.8	11.3	—	9.9
1964/65	12.8	12.2	—	10.8
1965/66	14.1	13.6	—	12.0
1966/67	15.6	15.0	—	13.3
1967/68	17.7	17.4	—	15.5
1968/69	18.7	18.2	—	16.1
1969/70	19.6	19.3	—	17.0
1970/71	22.1	21.6	—	19.1
1971/72	24.5	24.3	—	21.4
1972/73	28.1	27.6	—	24.8
1973/74	33.6	32.0	29.3	28.5
1974/75	44.9	42.8	39.4	38.6
1975/76	56.2	53.8	48.9	48.4
1976/77	63.3	59.6	54.5	53.2
1977/78	67.2	63.7	56.8	56.0
1978/79	77.7	74.8	65.8	65.3
1979/80	92.3	89.8	77.0	77.5
1980/81	111.7	108.4	92.7	93.3
1981/82	123.4	120.1	104.7	104.4
1982/83	136.3	132.6	113.4	114.6
1983/84	145.5	140.1	120.3	120.4
1984/85	153.6	149.5	129.7	128.7

[1]Public corporations market and overseas borrowing.

Table A.2 *Measures of public spending (in real terms)* [1]

	Pre-1977 public expenditure definition	General government expenditure	1985 planning total definition	1985 planning total definition excluding PCMOB [2]
1963/64	76.0	72.8	—	63.7
1964/65	78.7	75.3	—	66.5
1965/66	83.1	79.9	—	70.8
1966/67	87.8	84.7	—	75.1
1967/68	97.2	95.5	—	85.2
1968/69	97.6	95.1	—	84.3
1969/70	97.4	95.7	—	84.5
1970/71	101.2	98.9	—	87.5
1971/72	102.8	102.0	—	90.0
1972/73	109.3	107.4	—	96.4
1973/74	121.7	116.0	106.1	103.4
1974/75	136.3	130.1	119.5	117.2
1975/76	135.9	130.1	118.1	117.0
1976/77	135.1	127.2	116.3	113.6
1977/78	126.0	119.5	106.6	105.0
1978/79	131.9	126.9	111.7	110.9
1979/80	134.6	131.0	112.3	112.9
1980/81	137.3	133.2	113.9	114.7
1981/82	138.0	134.3	117.0	116.7
1982/83	142.6	138.7	118.6	119.9
1983/84	145.5	140.1	120.3	120.4
1984/85	147.0	143.1	124.2	123.3

[1] Cash figures divided by GDP deflator. 1983/84 = 100
[2] Public corporations market and overseas borrowing

Table A.3 *Definitions of debt interest payments (cash)*

£billion

	Public sector gross	General government gross	Public sector net
1973/74	3.3	3.0	0.5
1974/75	4.2	3.7	0.6
1975/76	5.1	4.6	0.9
1976/77	6.4	5.7	1.3
1977/78	7.2	6.5	1.8
1978/79	8.3	7.6	2.3
1979/80	10.5	9.8	3.4
1980/81	12.6	11.8	4.4
1981/82	14.6	13.9	5.7
1982/83	15.3	14.4	5.8
1983/84	15.4	14.9	7.1
1984/85	17.0	16.5	8.5

Table A.4 *Measures of public expenditure as a percentage of GDP*

percentage of GDP

	Pre-1977 public expenditure definition	General government expenditure	1985 planning total definition[2]	1985 planning total definition excluding PCMOB[1]	General government expenditure on goods and services
1963/64	37.3	36.8	—	33.6	20.4
1964/65	37.0	35.4	—	33.4	20.2
1965/66	38.3	36.8	—	34.5	20.8
1966/67	39.8	38.4	—	35.9	21.7
1967/68	42.7	42.0	—	39.4	22.7
1968/69	41.6	40.6	—	37.7	22.0
1969/70	40.6	40.0	—	36.9	21.5
1970/71	41.3	40.3	—	37.0	22.2
1971/72	41.2	40.8	—	37.4	22.4
1972/73	41.4	40.7	—	37.8	22.3
1973/74	44.6	42.5	40.4	39.4	23.8
1974/75	50.1	47.9	45.5	44.6	25.6
1975/76	50.6	48.5	45.7	45.3	26.5
1976/77	48.8	46.0	43.9	42.9	25.4
1977/78	44.5	42.3	39.7	39.1	23.3
1978/79	45.0	43.3	40.2	40.0	22.6
1979/80	44.6	43.4	39.7	39.9	22.4
1980/81	47.4	46.0	42.2	42.5	24.0
1981/82	47.6	46.3	43.5	43.4	23.5
1982/83	48.0	46.7	43.0	43.5	23.7
1983/84	47.6	45.8	42.6	42.7	23.6
1984/85	47.0	45.8	43.3	43.0	23.8

[1] Public corporations market and overseas borrowing
[2] As defined for the public expenditure GDP percentage in the 1985 PEWP

Table **A.5** *The link between the three definitions of public expenditure*

percentage of GDP

	General government expenditure	National accounts adjustments	Additional debt interest[1]	Public expenditure[2]	LA VAT and non-trading consumption	Public sector net debt interest	1985 planning total
1973/74	42.5	− 1.2	3.3	40.4	0.8	0.7	38.9
1974/75	47.9	− 1.1	3.5	45.5	0.8	0.7	44.0
1975/76	48.5	− 0.5	3.3	45.7	0.9	0.8	44.0
1976/77	46.0	− 1.3	3.4	43.9	0.9	1.0	42.0
1977/78	42.3	− 0.5	3.1	39.7	0.8	1.2	37.7
1978/79	43.3	—	3.1	40.2	0.8	1.3	38.1
1979/80	43.4	0.6	3.1	39.7	0.9	1.6	37.2
1980/81	46.0	0.5	3.2	42.2	0.9	1.9	39.3
1981/82	46.3	− 0.5	3.2	43.5	1.0	2.2	40.4
1982/83	46.7	0.6	3.1	43.0	1.0	2.0	40.0
1983/84	45.8	0.7	2.5	42.6	1.0	2.3	39.3
1984/85	45.8	− 0.1	2.6	43.3	1.0	2.6	39.7

[1] General government gross less public sector net
[2] As defined for public expenditure/GDP percentage in the 1985 PEWP

Table A.6 *The financing of general government expenditure*

percentage of GDP

	General government expenditure	GGBR[1]	Interest and dividends etc	Other receipts	National insurance and other contributions	Taxation
1963/64	35.8	3.2	1.3	2.5	4.3	24.5
1964/65	35.4	2.6	1.3	2.5	4.2	24.8
1965/66	36.8	2.5	1.4	2.0	4.7	26.2
1966/77	38.4	3.0	1.5	2.1	4.7	27.1
1967/68	42.0	5.0	1.6	2.3	4.8	28.3
1968/69	40.6	0.8	1.6	3.2	4.9	30.1
1969/70	40.0	-0.8	1.7	2.4	4.8	31.9
1970/71	40.3	1.0	1.7	1.4	5.0	31.2
1971/72	40.8	1.9	1.8	2.5	5.0	29.6
1972/73	40.7	3.6	1.8	3.0	5.1	27.2
1973/74	42.5	4.8	2.0	2.6	5.5	27.6
1974/75	47.9	8.2	2.1	2.0	6.0	29.6
1975/76	48.5	9.0	2.0	1.3	6.5	29.7
1976/77	46.0	5.6	1.9	2.7	6.8	29.0
1977/78	42.3	3.3	1.9	2.5	6.5	28.1
1978/79	43.3	5.2	1.7	2.7	5.9	27.8
1979/80	43.4	5.0	1.7	1.8	5.8	29.1
1980/81	46.0	5.8	1.7	2.6	6.1	29.8
1981/82	46.3	3.3	1.8	2.5	6.4	32.3
1982/83	46.7	3.6	1.9	2.7	6.6	31.9
1983/84	45.8	3.3	1.6	2.6	7.0	31.3
1984/85	45.8	2.9		3.9	6.9	32.1

[1]General government borrowing requirement.

Notes

1. P. Stibbard, 'Measuring Public Expenditure', *Economic Trends*, August 1985, has been especially helpful in compiling this annex.
2. The capital spending of a few small public corporations is still retained in public expenditure presumably because of their dependence upon central funding. See *1986 PEWP*, Cmnd. 9701–II, p. 399. A detailed explanation of the relationship between public corporation financing and the public expenditure total is contained in D. R. Steel and D. A. Heald, 'Integration of Public Enterprise and Exchequer Finances: Unravelling Dangerous Myth', *Public Administration*, vol. 62, no. 3, 1984, pp. 337–48.
3. Negative spending includes sales of capital assets.

Annex 2   Cost–Benefit Studies in the Public Sector

Chapter 4 made the point that there is a substantial literature covering the activities of Government Departments, much of it devoted to cost–benefit analysis studies. It is therefore possible to proceed on the assumption that benefit–cost ratios are available over a reasonably wide range of governmental activities. There are some obvious gaps, such as defence. However, in many such areas, even if there were usable benefit–cost ratios it is probable that non-economic considerations would largely dictate resource allocation. In other words, where the practical applications of the technique are clearly going to be few economists have not devoted many resources to those ends.

A general survey of the use of cost–benefit analysis in British Government, which includes some lengthy case studies, is P. Colvin, *The Economic Ideal in British Government* (Manchester University Press, 1985). The research on which Colvin's book is based is now somewhat dated but it was reviewed by an anonymous contributor to *Public Money* in June 1986 'Evaluating Government Activity: The Limits of Cost–Benefit Analysis and Other Techniques' in the course of which several interesting points were made. While claiming that the various economic effects of government activity can be given monetary values economists have always conceded that the ultimate stage of analysis:

> valuing the different impacts (or outputs) of policy, was inescapably not value-free. That was particularly true when it came to adding up positive and negative outputs, and setting gainers off against losers. As a rule this stage of policy evaluation is carried out on the basis of political judgement. (*Public Money*, June 1986, p. 59).

Although much progress has been made in giving monetary values to, for example, environmental impacts, gains and losses of amenity value, and so on, there is a problem at the heart of some cost–benefit studies concerned with the distributional impact of gains and losses.

It is not the intention of this annex to gloss over that problem. It does exist. No amount of technique will make it go away. However, its existence does not invalidate the use of CBA techniques. Although the final calculation of values will never be a value-free process, because of the distributional problem, it should not be concluded that the elements of CBA:

● the systematic identification of alternative options
● the quantification of physical impacts
● the monetary evaluation of those impacts
● the setting of monetary values in a consistent time framework
● and the assessment of major uncertainties

are therefore an unnecessary encumbrance in the decision-making process.

A similar lapse of logic assails those who seek to invalidate CBA on the grounds that for certain cost and benefit categories, notably injury and fatality costs, there are wide ranges of possible values. The point seems to be either that the world is uncertain (which affects all decision-making processes without implying that no decisions should be taken) or that, *by assumption*, loss of life, or destruction of rustic quietude, or whatever, should not be valued – an article of faith we are free to reject.

It should be clear from the above that this is an area about which there is some controversy. With that caveat in mind the following listing of published CBA studies is offered. These studies do not constitute the entire body of literature as many substantial works have been generated internally by departmental economists or have been commissioned from external consultants but never published. The listing is restricted to works published in the past decade or so.

Agriculture

J. R. Crabtree, 'The Appraisal of Machinery Investment', *Journal of Agricultural Economics*, September 1981.

A. P. Power and K. S. Warwick, 'An Approach to the Measurement of the Cost and Benefits of Poultry Meat Inspection', *Proceedings of the Society for Veterinary Epidemiology and Preventive Medicines*, Annual Conference, Edinburgh, July 1984.

Education

G. Psacharopoulos, 'Returns to Education: an Updated International Comparison', *Comparative Education*, vol. 17, no. 3, 1981.

R. A. Wilson, 'The Rate of Return to becoming a Qualified Scientist or Engineer in Great Britain, 1966–76', *Scottish Journal of Political Economy*, vol. 21, no. 1, 1980.

R. A. Wilson, 'Rates of Return – Some Further Results', *SJPE*, vol. 30, no. 2, 1983.

R. A. Wilson, 'A Longer Perspective on Rates of Return', *SJPE*, vol. 32, no. 2, 1985.

R. A. Wilson, 'The Social Returns to Producing Teachers', *Higher Education Review*, vol. 17, no. 3, 1985.

R. A. Wilson, 'The Declining Return to Becoming a Teacher', *Higher Education Review*, vol. 15, Summer 1983.

G. Williams and A. Gordon, 'Perceived Earnings Functions and Ex Ante Rates of Return to Post-Compulsory Education in England', *Higher Education*, vol. 10, 1981.

Employment

P. Colvin, *The Economic Ideal in British Government* (Manchester University Press, 1985). Chapter 5 on the CBA of Skillcentre training.

B. Deakin and C. Pratten *Effects of the Temporary Employment Subsidy* (Cambridge University Press, 1982).

P. S. Johnson and R. B. Thomas, 'Government Policies Towards Business Formation: An Economic Appraisal of a Training Scheme', *Scottish Journal of Political Economy, 1*, vol. 31, no. 2, June 1984.

R. Layard, 'The Costs and Benefits of Selective Employment

Policies: The British Case', *British Journal of Industrial Relations*, vol. 17, 1979, pp. 187–204.

P. Morgan, 'The Costs and Benefits of the Power Presses Regulations (1985)', *British Journal of Industrial Relations*, July 1983.

A. Ziderman, 'Costs and Benefits of Manpower Training Programmes in Great Britain', *British Journal of Industrial Relations*, vol. 13, 1975.

Energy

Severn Barrage Committee, *Tidal Power from the Severn Estuary*, vol. 2, Energy Paper no. 46 (London: HMSO, 1981).

Energy Technology Support Unit, *Strategic Review of the Energy Technologies: An Economic Assessment*, vol. II, ETSU R. 13, November 1982.

N. Evans and C. Hope, *Nuclear Power: Futures, Costs and Benefits* (Cambridge University Press, 1984), Chapter 8.

N. Evans, *The Sizewell Decision: A Sensitivity Analysis*, Energy Research Group, University of Cambridge, Cavendish Laboratory, ERG 83/11.

F. P. Jenkin, *The Need for Sizewell B* (London, CEGB, 1982). This was part of the evidence to the Sizewell enquiry. Evidence no. CEGB/P/4.

Environment

M. A. Cohen, 'The Costs and Benefits of Oil Spill Prevention and Enforcement', *Journal of Environmental Economics and Management*, vol. 13, No. 2, June 1986.

A. D. J. Flowerdew and F. Rodriguez, *The Effect of Urban Renewal on Residents' Benefits and Social Welfare: A Case Study* (London, Centre for Environmental Studies, 1978) Research Series, no. 24.

D. W. Pearce and R. Kerry Turner, 'Cost–Benefit Analysis in Practice, II: The Social Appraisal of Materials Recycling' in D. W. Pearce and C. A. Nash, *The Social Appraisal of Projects* (London: Macmillan, 1981) and references cited therein.

T. Young and P. G. Allen, 'Methods for Valuing Countryside Amenity: An Overview', *Journal of Agricultural Economics*, vol. 37, no. 3, Sept 1986.

Health

M. Buxton and R. West, 'Cost–Benefit Analysis of Long Term Haemodialysis for Chronic Renal Failure', *British Medical Journal*, 17 May 1975.

A. T. Culyer, 'Health Service Efficiency – Appraising the Appraisers', *University of York, Centre for Health Economics, Discussion Paper no 10*, September 1985.

M. F. Drummond, *Studies in Economic Appraisal in Health Care* (Oxford: Oxford Medical Publications, 1980).

G. Ginsberg and I. M. Marks, 'Costs and Benefits of Behavioural Psychotherapy: A Pilot Study of Neurotics Treated by Nurse Therapists', *Psychological Medicine* vol. 7, 1977, pp. 685–700

N. Glass and D. Goldberg, 'Cost–Benefit Analysis and the Evaluation of Psychiatric Services', *Psychological Medicine*, vol. 7, 1977, pp. 701–7.

D. Goldberg and R. Jones, 'The Costs and Benefits of Psychiatric Care', in L. Robins, P. Clayton and J. K. Wing (eds) *The Social Consequences of Psychiatric Illness* (New York: Brunner/Mazel, 1980) pp. 55–70.

S. Hagard, F. Carter and R. G. Milne, 'Screening for Spina Bifida Cystica: A Cost–Benefit Analysis', *British Journal of Preventive and Social Medicine*, vol. 38, 1976.

R. Jones, D. Goldberg and B. Hughes, 'A Comparison of Two Different Services Treating Schizophrenia: A Cost–Benefit Approach', *Psychological Medicine*, vol. 10, 1980, pp. 493–505.

G. H. Mooney, 'Values in Health Care' in K. Lee (ed.) *Economics and Health Planning* (London: Croom Helm, 1979).

G. H. Mooney, *The Valuation of Human Life* (London: Macmillan, 1977).

B. A. Weisbrod, M. A. Test and L. I. Stein, 'Alternatives to Mental Hospital Treatment II: Economic Benefit–Cost Analysis', *Archives of General Psychiatry*, vol. 37, 1980, pp. 400–5.

B. A. Weisbrod, 'Benefit–Cost Analysis of a Controlled Experiment: Treating the Mentally Ill', *Journal of Human Resources*, vol. XVI, no. 4, 1981, pp. 523–48.

A. H. Williams, 'The Costs and Benefits of Surgery' in J. S. P. Lumley and J. L. Craven (eds) *Surgical Review I* (London: Butterworths, 1978).

Industry

S. J. Cameron *et al.*, *Local Authority Aid to Industry: An Evaluation in Tyne and Wear* (London, DOE, 1982).
F. Herron, 'An Economic Assessment of the Effects of Selective Assistance under the Industry Act 1972', *Government Economic Service Working Paper no. 84*, DTI 1986.
I. D. Hodge and M. C. Whitby, 'New Jobs in the Eastern Borders: An Economic Evaluation of the Development Commission Factory Programmes', *University of Newcastle upon Tyne: Agricultural Adjustment Unit, Monograph 8*, 1979.
M. C. Whitby and K. G. Willis, *New Jobs in Mid-Wales* (New Town Development Board for Rural Wales, 1983).

Overseas development

G. A. Bridger and J. T. Winpenny, *Planning Development Projects: A Practical Guide to the Choice and Appraisal of Public Sector Investments* (London: HMSO, 1983) sets out in some detail how the ODA goes about appraising projects.

Transport

There are very many sources of information; a recently published account of practice in the Department of Transport is contained in P. Colvin, *The Economic Ideal in British Government* (Manchester University Press, 1985) Chapter 4. See also the footnotes to that chapter, pp. 211–16, for a listing of sources.

Welfare

M. Knapp, *The Economics of Social Care* (London: Macmillan, 1984). Chapter 8 concerns CBA in the context of residential and community care of the elderly.

Glossary of Terms and Acronyms

AS: Autumn Statement.

Borrowing from Money Markets: Governments require funds to finance spending. To the extent that funds are not provided by taxes, the National Insurance Fund, interest receipts, etc, they are borrowed. Such borrowing can either be by the selling of *gilt edged securities* (see below) to the non-bank sector (private individuals, pension funds, corporations); or by placing Treasury Bills with the banking sector or through National Savings.

Constant Prices: If the prices used in a statistical series all refer to one particular point in time, for example, a year, they are said to be in constant prices. For example, all prices might be expressed in 'constant 1985/86 prices'. To achieve that object values before 1985/86 would need to be *inflated* by the amount of price inflation observed, and values after 1985/86 would need to be *deflated* by the amount of price inflation experienced. See also: *Deflators*, *Real Terms* and *Survey Prices*.

Demand-Led Spending: Once the Government has stated the terms on which certain funds may be obtained – for example, pensions, unemployment benefit, housing improvement grants, etc – the amount of spending depends entirely upon demand. For some kinds of such demand-led spending the rate at which applications are processed may be under direct government control. In this case government may influence the rate of spending, for example, by allowing queues to lengthen.

Deflator: A statistical construct used to express values in the prices of a particular period. For example, if prices have an index value of 100 in period 1 and increase by 5 per cent between periods 1 and 2 they will have an index value of 105 in period 2. If all period 2 prices are deflated using the deflator *1.05* they will thus be rendered into period 1 prices.

EC: European Community.

Economy: Loosely used in official language to mean frugality or sensible parsimony. More formally, we may distinguish between Planned Inputs (PI) and Actual Inputs (AI). Then PI/AI will be a ratio measure of economy.

Effectiveness: The extent to which the aims and objectives of an organisation have been met. More formally, it can be supposed that Planned Output (PO) and Actual Output (AO) measure how effective an organisation is. However, the organisation may neglect some means of obtaining maximum effectiveness or Maximum Output (MO). Thus, even if AO/PO is greater than unity it may also be true that MO/AO is greater than unity. Unless PO is not significantly different from MO a rating of unity for PO/AO will not indicate maximum effectiveness. Finally, an organisation can be *effective* without being *efficient* – it may use more resources than are necessary.

Efficiency: The minimising of inputs in relation to outputs, or the maximising of outputs in relation to inputs. In ratio form Actual Output (AO) in relation to Actual Input (AI).

External Financing Limits (EFLs): Annual limits set on the ability of the nationalised industries and public corporations to raise money 'externally', that is, other than from their own internal resources. External finance consists of loans, overdrafts and the sale of debt instruments to the bank and non-bank sectors.

Financial Management Initiative (FMI): The initiative resulting from a paper issued by the Treasury and the Management and Personnel Office in May 1982, reprinted as Appendix 3 of Government Observations on the Third Report from the Treasury and Civil Service Committee, Session 1981/82, *Efficiency and Effectiveness in the Civil Service* (London: HMSO, September 1982), Cmnd. 8616. The paper began, 'The time has come for a general and co-ordinated drive to improve financial management in Government departments'. A report on the progress of the FMI is cited in the concluding chapter, note 5.

103

FSBR: Financial Statement and Budget Report.

Futures Markets: Such markets exist for the purchase or sale of commodities on a specified future date. They allow manufacturers and traders to protect themselves against a change in the price of commodities they use or deal in.

Gilt Edged Securities: Borrowing instruments used by Government to raise finance. They take the form of a certificate with a nominal value and a fixed nominal rate of interest; they may or may not be ultimately redeemable. They are called gilt edged because, backed by the Government's power to raise taxes, it is *certain* that interest will be paid and the instrument will be redeemed (where appropriate). As they are traded on the Stock Exchange they may fluctuate in value; thus the fixed nominal rate of interest can vary in real terms. Thus, assume a security issued at £100 with 5 per cent nominal interest. If the demand for such securities suddenly declines the price will fall and the £5 nominal interest will increase as a percentage yield. For example, if the price fell to £50 the interest would represent a 10 per cent yield. Because market expectations about future gilt edge prices are very much governed by the expected supply of securities (in turn influenced to a great degree by the PSBR) in relation to demand, an unexpectedly large PSBR will engender rising interest rates (all other things being equal).

Gross Domestic Product (GDP): A measure of the total flow of goods and services produced by the domestic economy during a period (usually a year, although official statistics are published quarterly). If we add together:

Private consumption
Government current expenditure
Gross domestic fixed capital formation
Value of increase in stocks and work in progress.

the sum is: *Domestic Expenditure at Market Prices*. Adding to this exports and subtracting imports gives: *Gross Domestic Product at market prices*. If indirect taxes are subtracted and subsidies added we have: *Gross Domestic Product at factor cost* (GDPfc). GDPfc plus net property income from abroad gives: *Gross National Product at factor cost* (GNPfc). GNPfc minus Capital Consumption gives *National Income*.

Opportunity Cost: The value of a resource in its next best alternative use. In economics this concept is distinguished from market price, which may not reflect alternative use value if imperfections exist. However, providing that no significant monopoly elements exist, that resources can be freely bid for, that taxes and subsidies can be adjusted for, and that prices are not otherwise artificially administered, market prices should reflect opportunity costs. Crucially, if a resource has no alternative use whatsoever its opportunity cost is zero.

PE: Public Expenditure.

PEPT: Public Expenditure Planning Total.

PES: Public Expenditure Survey.

PESC: Public Expenditure Survey Committee.

PEWP: Public Expenditure White Paper.

PSBR: Public Sector Borrowing Requirement.

Real Terms: This literally refers to the physical characteristics of goods and services as opposed to their money characteristics. As these physical attributes of goods and services cannot be compared directly, measurements in money terms are adjusted to an approximation of real terms by correcting for changes in money values. The procedure is analytically indistinguishable from that used in deriving a *constant price* series (see above): so 'constant prices' and 'real terms' are interchangeable expressions.

Relative Price Effect (RPE): The phenomenon whereby price inflation in sector X is systematically different from that observed in Sector Y. The RPE may be positive or negative. The cause of a positive RPE for the public sector, compared to the private sector or the domestic economy as a whole, has been attributed to: a) inferior *actual* productivity growth in the public sector and b) inferior *recorded* productivity growth in the public sector since, by national accounting convention, the rate of change in output cannot differ from the rate of change in input (the latter is used to proxy the former).

SGSE: Summary and Guide to the Supply Estimates.

Survey Prices: The *constant prices* (see above) used in the PES process prior to 1981. The particular base period used was the mid-November point of the year prior to the survey year, that is, two years prior to the Autumn of the first plan year.

TCSC: Treasury and Civil Service Committee.

Value for Money (VFM): A Treasury source states: 'This is usually interpreted as being some optimal combination of economy, efficiency and effectiveness, which are often referred to as "value for money" measures', (HM Treasury, *Output and Performance in Central Government: Progress in Departments*, Treasury Working Paper no. 38, February 1986). If PI/AI (see above: *Economy*) increases, all other things being equal, VFM increases. If AO/AI (see above: *Efficiency*) increases, all other things being equal, VFM increases. Also, if AO/PO (see above: *Effectiveness*) increases, all other things being equal, VFM increases. At any one point in time, of course, one of these ratios may be increasing while the other two ratios are decreasing: hence the reference to an 'optimal combination' of the three measures. However, it can readily be seen that the *Efficiency* measure is central to VFM because achieved increases in Economy (PI/AI) and Effectiveness (AO/PO) will both always imply increases in Efficiency (AO/AI). Effectiveness (AO/PO) and Economy (PI/AI), because they do not share terms, do not impact on one another. Therefore, the efficiency ratio acts as a summary measure. In this sense, VFM can be taken literally to mean the (if possible monetised) value of output per unit of monetised value of input.

Notes and References

Introduction

1. Annex 1 is wholly devoted to the various statistical definitions of public expenditure which have been employed in the past decade.
2. Central Statistical Office, *United Kingdom National Accounts, Sources and Methods*, 3rd edn (London: HMSO, 1985) ch. 5, sets out the methodological problem clearly. In theory, resource inputs in the public sector can move freely between the public and private sectors. At the margin, therefore, such resources will command incomes which reflect the value of output produced in the public sector. If they did not, they would be released by the public sector (incomes in excess of output values) or lured away by the private sector (output values in excess of incomes). Providing there is 'correct' marginal valuation of public sector resources their prices can act as a guide to output values in the public sector.
3. Hence, most of the definitions of public spending are improperly compared to GDP: financial transfers do not appear in GDP, nor do sales of state-owned capital assets, nor interest on debt instruments. See Annex 1 for more discussion of these points.
4. The concept of opportunity cost may be novel to some readers. See the Glossary for a short discussion.

1 From Plowden to Cash Planning

1. As the next section of this chapter is entirely devoted to the key documents in the history of public expenditure planning during 1961–1982 no source references will be cited in this overview.
2. See the Glossary entry under *Borrowing from Money Markets*. The point was that planning was in terms of constant prices unaffected by, and abstracting from, actual inflation. However, day-to-day spending had to be in cash terms. In periods of rapidly rising prices not having an explicit system taking into account cash demands meant that a most important problem in the practical management of public spending was dealt with, as it were, off-stage.
3. Broadly speaking, those programmes where spending was not demand-led and where Parliamentary approval for Estimates was

required (neither National Insurance Fund spending nor local authority rent and rates come within the compass of Estimates). Examples of demand-led spending include social security benefits, agricultural support payments to the European Community, university student awards and General Practitioner payments.

4. See, for example, the discussion in D. Heald, *Public Expenditure* (Oxford: Martin Robertson, 1983), p. 194.
5. For an extended technical description of cash limits see A. Likierman, *Cash Limits and External Financing Limits* (London: HMSO, 1981) Civil Service College Handbook, no. 22.
6. Her Majesty's Treasury, *Economic Progress Report*, November 1981, no. 139, p. 2.
7. For a more elaborate and technical description see Cmnd. 8494, 1982, vol II, p. 103. The actual cash plans in each of the three years were additionally adjusted for a higher than expected police pay settlement in September 1981.
8. Her Majesty's Treasury, *Economic Progress Report*, March 1981; see also Her Majesty's Treasury, *Financial Statement and Budget Report*, March 1981.
9. S. Lewis and A. Harrison, 'How Real are Real Terms Resources?', *Public Money*, September 1983, p. 54.
10. D. Heald, *Public Expenditure* (Oxford: Martin Robertson, 1983), p. 196.

2   The public expenditure planning process

1. For example

	1986/87	1987/88	1988/89	1989/90
1985 Survey	1	2	3	—
1986 Survey	—	1	2	3

2. Reduced requirements may arise from: (i) increased efficiency; (ii) the lapsing of an activity, for example, the end of a research programme, or the abolition of a statute; (iii) privatisation, or contracting out, of a departmental activity; (iv) falling demand as population declines; (v) revised economic assumptions concerning prices and interest rates, etc, which affect demand-led programmes.
3. S. Jenkins, 'The Star Chamber, PESC and the Cabinet', *Political Quarterly*, vol. 56, no. 2, 1985. The 1984 Star Chamber was composed of Lord Whitelaw, the leader of the House (John Biffen), the Scottish Secretary (George Younger) and the Home Secretary (Leon Brittan).
4. All Departments now have such systems for reviewing objectives, inputs and outputs as a result of the Financial Management Initiative (FMI) which dates from 1982. Following the FMI departments introduced financial management accounting techniques. A useful review of the early years is contained in *Progress in Financial Management in Government* (London: HMSO, 1984) Cmnd. 9297.

See also Peat, Marwick, Mitchell and Co., *Financial Management in the Public Sector, A Review 1979/84* (London: Peat Marwick Mitchell, 1985)

5. For example, both the 1983 and 1984 PEWPs were published in February; that for 1981 was published in March.

6. Department of the Environment, *Paying for Local Government* (London: HMSO, 1986) Cmnd. 9714, pp. 83–90 gives more detail, although very little flavour of the politically sensitive nature of the changes introduced during the 1980s.

7. Eighth Report from the Treasury and Civil Service Committee, Session 1980/81, *Financing of the Nationalised Industries*, (London: HMSO, 1981) HC. 348–I, volume I, p. xiii.

8. H. Heclo and A. Wildavsky, *The Private Government of Public Money* (London: Macmillan; 1981, 2nd edn), p. 91, where the technique is called the 'beggar's sores technique'.

9. C. Ponting, *Whitehall: Tragedy and Farce* (London: Hamish Hamilton, 1986). The quotation cited is from B. Castle, *The Castle Diaries* (London: Weidenfeld & Nicolson, 1980), p. 596. Lord Bruce Gardyne, an ex-Treasury Minister, has observed: 'What is too often overlooked though is the ingrained conviction of the Whitehall mandarins that the size of their respective departmental budgets is a matter of personal machismo. It doesn't matter what the money is to be used for; its the amount of the money that matters', *Sunday Telegraph*, 30 November 1986.

10. A. Likierman, 'Squaring the Circle: Reconciling Predictive Uncertainty with the Control of Public Expenditure in the UK', *Policy and Politics*, vol. 14, July 1986, p. 291.

11. An official version of this narrative may be consulted in Cabinet Office/HM Treasury, *Government Accounting: Public Expenditure Survey* (London: HMSO, 1985), prepared by Peter Saunders Associates, Liss Forest, Hants.

12. PESC is the Public Expenditure Survey Committee composed of the Principal Finance Officers of departments and chaired by a Treasury deputy secretary. It used to be very active in surveying the data forwarded by departments during the PES; now, it does not even rate a mention in official descriptions of the cycle. See HM Treasury, *The Management of Public Spending* (London: GEPG, 1986) paras 9–20.

3 Public spending documentation

1. Lord Armstrong, *Budgeting Reform in the United Kingdom* (Oxford: Oxford University Press, for the Institute for Fiscal Studies, 1980).

2. In the main such criticism has been voiced by the House of Commons, Treasury and Civil Service Committee. See, for example, the Sixth Report from the T&CSC, Session 1984/85, *The Government's Expenditure Plans 1985/86 to 1987/88* (25 February 1985, HC 213), p. viii ff.

3. Similarly, for 1986/87 the GDP deflator was expected to increase by 4½ per cent. Thus, to get to the 1984/85 base we have: £139.1/ 1.045 = £133.11/1.05 = £126.77 billions.
4. The perhaps more familiar GNP or *Gross National Product* is GDP plus net property income from abroad. See the Glossary for a fuller discussion.
5. National Audit Office, *Financial Reporting to Parliament* (London: HMSO, 1986) HC 576, p. 13.
6. Ibid, p. 3.
7. The description used for the Arts and Libraries indicators in 1985: HM Treasury, *The Government's Expenditure Plans, 1985/86 to 1987/ 88* (London: HMSO, January 1985, Cmnd. 9428–II) p. 91.
8. Ibid, pp. 125–6.
9. Cmnd. 9702–II, p. 394. The 1987 PEWP has moved this statement to the beginning of the second volume: *PEWP 1987*, Cmnd. 56–II, para I.
10. See, for example, the *Armstrong Report*, and D. Heald, *Public Expenditure* (Oxford: Martin Robertson, 1983), pp 197–8.
11. The Armstrong Report employs two further arguments: (a) without early indication of a budget constraint on spending, ministers 'spend up' and disruptive cuts are made later; (b) the last minute nature of Budget tax changes means that no coherent strategy (for example, on the balance of direct and indirect tax burdens) is considered. See the *Armstrong Report*, pp. 9–10.
12. For more on the Estimates system the interested reader can refer to: House of Commons, Sixth Report from the Treasury and Civil Service Committee, Session 1980/81, 'The Form of the Estimates', July 1981, HC 325; and: HM Treasury, *The Management of Public Spending* (London: GEPG, May 1986).
13. Sixth Report 1984/85, p. xviii.
14. Second Report from the T&CSC, 1986/87, *The Government's Economic Policy: Autumn Statement* (London: HMSO, 1986) HC 27.
15. Third Report from the Treasury and Civil Service Committee, Session 1985/86, *The Government's Expenditure Plans 1986/87 to 1988/89 (Cmnd. 9702)* para 21, p. x.
16. See, for example, the *Daily Telegraph*, 17 July 1986, 'Lawson Ready To Ease The Purse Strings'. Departmental bids were said to exceed the inherited PES total of £144 billions by £7 billions.
17. HM Treasury, *The Next Ten Years: Public Expenditure and Taxation into the 1980s* (London: HMSO, 1984, Cmnd. 9189).
18. A. Likierman and P. Vass, *Structure and Form of Government Expenditure Reports: Proposals for Reform* (London: Certified Accountants Publications, 1984); or, for a review of its contents and some repercussions: P. Vass, 'The Agenda for Reform of United Kingdom Government Expenditure Reports', *Financial Accountability and Management*, Winter 1985, pp. 101–12.
19. NAO, *Financial Reporting to Parliament*.

4 The Role of the Treasury

1. B. Castle, *The Castle Diaries* (London: Weidenfeld & Nicolson, 1980), p. 481. The political memoirs of ex-Cabinet member Jim Prior make clear that the July Cabinet is mainly concerned with the balance of macroeconomic policy. See 'Margaret As Manager', *The Observer*, 28 September 1986, p. 21.
2. J. Barnett, *Inside The Treasury* (London: André Deutsch, 1982), p. 59.
3. L. Pliatzky, *Paying and Choosing* (Oxford: Basil Blackwell, 1985). Chapter 1 expounds this argument at some length.
4. A similar tabulation appears in the 1986 PEWP, Cmnd. 9702–I, p. 20.
5. Apart from the sources already noted this chapter draws upon the following: D. Wass, *Government and the Governed: BBC Reith Lectures 1983* (London: Routledge & Kegan Paul, 1984); Sir D. Henley, *et al.*, *Public Sector Accounting and Financial Control* (Wokingham: Van Nostrand Reinhold, 1983); L. Pliatzky, *Getting and Spending* (Oxford: Basil Blackwell, rev. edn, 1984); H. Young and A. Sloman, *But Chancellor* (London, BBC, 1984); Sir S. Goldman, *The Developing System of Public Expenditure Management and Control* (London: HMSO, 1973); C. Ham, *Health Policy in Britain* (London, Macmillan: 1985, rev. edn).
6. See Third Report from the Treasury and Civil Service Committee, 1980/81, *Monetary Policy*, vol 1, Report, 24 February 1981, (London: HMSO, HC 163–1) pp. xxxii–xliii, for a description of four schools of thought on economic policy.
7. See the remarks of Sir Anthony Rawlinson and Nicholas Monck in H. Young and A. Sloman, *But Chancellor*, p. 44, and p. 45.
8. More formally (where MV = Marginal Value and MC = Marginal Cost in a two good world) if: MV_1/MC_1 is greater than MV_2/MC_2 total value can be increased by buying less of good 2 and more of good 1. If however, $MV_1/MC_1 = MV_2/MC_2$ it is not possible to increase value by rearranging purchases.
9. See Peter Middleton's remarks in Young and Sloman, *But Chancellor*, p. 62.
10. S. Jenkins, 'The Star Chamber, PESC and the Cabinet', *Political Quarterly*, vol. 56, no. 2, 1985.
11. On this and related issues see Diana Seammen in Young and Sloman, *But Chancellor*, p. 49; Frank Cooper, loc. cit. p. 47; Lord Bridges, *The Treasury* (London: Allen and Unwin, 1964) pp. 51–3; H. Heclo and A. Wildavsky *The Private Government of Public Money*, pp. 82–4; Sir S. Goldman, *The Developing System of Public Expenditure Management and Control*, p. 39.
12. First Report, Treasury and Civil Service Committee, Session 1984/85 *The Government's Economic Policy: Autumn Statement* (London: HMSO, HC 44) p. 45, para. 312.
13. J. Barnett, *Inside the Treasury*, p. 155; and D. Healey in Young and Sloman, *But Chancellor*, p. 64.

14. L. Pliatzky, *Paying and Choosing*, p. 42. Such reviews are also alluded to in HM Treasury, *The Management of Public Spending*, para. 74.

15. L. Pliatzky, Ibid., pp. 52–55. During the early 1970s the CPRS prepared a joint paper with Treasury on public expenditure priorities at the start of each PES round. Between 1974/79 this paper was

15. prepared by CPRS alone. The Cabinet's inability to take an informed view on departmental priorities is thoroughly discussed in: P. Hennessy *Cabinet* (Oxford: Basil Blackwell, 1986) pp. 189–91.

16. L. Pliatzky, *Paying and Choosing*, pp. 47–51.

17. It is symptomatic of Pliatzky's treatment that to support his argument he recalls *one* CBA (of the forestry programme) conducted in *1972*.

18. There are several useful CBA primers: E. J. Mishan, *Cost–Benefit Analysis* (London: Allen and Unwin, 3rd. edn, 1982); L. G. Anderson and R. F. Settle, *Benefit–Cost Analysis: A Practical Guide* (Lexington Books, 1978); D. W. Pearce (ed.) *The Valuation of Social Cost* (London: Allen & Unwin, 1978); D. W. Pearce, *Cost–Benefit Analysis* (London: St. Martin, 1983). The use of CBA in the public sector is outlined in HM Treasury, *Investment Appraisal In the Public Sector: A Technical Guide for Government Departments* (London: HMT, 1984).

19. G. H. Mooney, *Economics, Medicine and Health Care* (Brighton: Wheatsheaf, 1986) pp. 58–71. See Note 8 above. If the equality $MV_1/MC_1 = MV_2/MC_2$ holds then the equality $MV_1/MV_2 = MC_1/MC_2$ also holds. Thus if marginal costs are known the relative order of values is known. Of course, inspection of such ratios illuminates whether programme managers *have* arrived at the optimal allocation of resources.

20. D. Pearce, G. Mooney, R. Akehurst and P. West, 'Rational Establishment of Air Quality Standards', *Environmental Health Perspectives*, vol. 52, 1983.

21. G. Davies and D. Metcalf, 'The Cost of Generating Jobs', *The Economics Analyst* (London: Simon & Coates, 9 April 1985).

22. That is: (a) Do the stated benefit–cost ratios hold if inter-dependent projects are undertaken? (b) Do the stated benefit–cost ratios hold if £x or 10£x is spent?

23. For a lively survey of this and related issues: S. E. Rhoads, *The Economist's View of the World* (Cambridge: Cambridge University Press, 1985). Also D. W. Pearce and C. A. Nash, *The Social Appraisal of Projects* (London: MacMillan, 1981); and J. A. Sinden and A. C. Worrell, *Unpriced Values* (New York: John Wiley, 1979).

24. See A. T. O'Donnell and T. E. Rhodes, *Risk, Uncertainty and Public Sector Investment Appraisal*, HM Treasury, Government Economic Service W. P. no. 63, September 1983, p. 33 ff; and HM Treasury, *Investment Appraisal in the Public Sector* 1984, paras. 3.49–3.52.

5   Resource Planning

1. The ground will be familiar to economists. General readers may wish to consult M. H. Peston, *The British Economy: An Elementary Macroeconomic Perspective* (Deddington: Philip Allan, 1982) and C. Hawkins & G. McKenzie, *The British Economy* (London: MacMillan, 1982).
2. The facts are:

	Percentage annual rate of inflation	Percentage annual unemployment rate
1950s	4.1*	1.2
1960s	4.0	1.6
1970s	13.8	3.5

*2.8% if 1950 and 1951 are omitted.

Source: *Economic Trends*, Annual Supplement, 1986.

3. The price series used is the all items retail price index. The unemployment rate is total unemployed including school leavers as a percent of the working population.

3. Peston, *The British Economy: An Elementary Macroeconomic Perspective*, p. 147, has expressed this succinctly: 'It should not be forgotten that fiscal and monetary policy are interrelated. An increase in public expenditure or a cut in taxation will initially tend to raise the government's budget deficit. If the government borrows long term to finance this, interest rates may rise, and some private expenditure (that part sensitive to higher interest rates) will fall. Short term government borrowing, at the other extreme, adds to the money supply, in that it provides reserve assets for the commercial banks. The result will again be seen to be more inflation.'
4. For example, because unions would be aware that expanding demand gave rise to increased profits this would prompt them to ask for higher money wages; also, entrepreneurs would anticipate similar pressures on firms supplying them with intermediate goods. The end result would be a mix of higher prices and increased output. Thus the output response to increased demand pressure would be dampened.
5. HM Treasury, *Public Expenditure in 1963/64 and 1967/68* (London: HMSO, December 1963) Cmnd. 2235, para. 34.
6. HM Treasury, *Public Expenditure: Planning and Control* (London: HMSO, February 1966) Cmnd. 2915, para. 15. The quotation referred to events in January 1965 when a growth rate of 4¼ per cent per annum for public expenditure was derived in this way.
7. HM Treasury, *Public Expenditure in 1968/69 and 1969/70* (London: HMSO, January 1968) Cmnd. 3515, para. 3.
8. The main events are lucidly surveyed by C. T. Sandford, *National*

Economic Planning (London: Heinemann, 1972), Chapter 5.

9. Even with HM Treasury, *The Attack on Inflation* (London: HMSO, July 1975) Cmnd. 6151, para. 43, it was stated: 'The paramount need to move resources into exports and investment makes it essential to contain the demands on resources made by public expenditure programmes.'

10. Having published resource planning tables during 1972/76 the table in Cmnd. 6393 was the last one to appear in a PEWP.

11. In R. Klein and M. O'Higgins (eds) *The Future of Welfare* (Oxford: Basil Blackwell, 1985), p. 94.

12. About the average level of GDP growth in the UK, 1950/85.

13. HM Treasury, *The Next Ten Years: Public Expenditure and Taxation into the 1980s* (London: HMSO, 1984, Cmnd. 9189), passim.

14. For the sake of argument we are assuming that Keynesian policies of demand management can have some effect on demand and output in the short run.

15. A classic example was the contrast between the growth assumptions in Table 5.2 for the years beyond 1975 and the 'standstill' policies adopted in 1976 after the Sterling crisis of that year.

16. See J. E. Meade, *The Theory of Indicative Planning* (Manchester University Press, 1970) and *The Intelligent Radical's Guide to Economic Policy* (London: Allen & Unwin, 1975), Chapter VII.

17. 'Futures markets': see the Glossary.

18. They are as yet unborn or are still at school.

19. Shortages would hamper growth, while unwanted surpluses would disappoint entrepreneurial expectations and, by reaction, may lead to future shortages.

20. Political and Economic Planning, *Growth in the British Economy* (London: Allen & Unwin, 1960), p. 24.

21. A. Budd, *The Politics of Economic Planning* (Glasgow: Fontana/ Collins, 1978), Chapters 5–7.

22. See C. T. Sandford, *National Economic Planning*, Chapters 4 & 5.

6 The Advent of Cash Planning

1. HM Treasury, *Economic Progress Report*, no. 139, November 1981, p. 1.

2. The impression given by P. Mountfield, 'Recent Developments in the Control of Public Expenditure in the United Kingdom', *Public Finance Quarterly*, Fall 1983.

3. 'Classical' economics, 'classical' model and 'classical' analysis are used here to refer to the pre-Keynesian state of affairs in economic understanding. The Classicists, extant in the nineteenth century, generally held that markets would prevent severe recession emerging. Some Classical economists, for example Malthus, supplemented this with an interest rate mechanism whereby investment demand was

stimulated when savings increased and interest rates declined. Marshall is usually taken to be the last great Classical economist although he absorbed the newer marginalist ideas of Jevons and others.

4. Any standard textbook may be consulted. A clear treatment is given in D. G. Pierce and P. J. Tysome, *Monetary Economics* (London: Butterworths, 1985) 2nd edn. pp. 40–5.

5. M. Friedman, *Essays in Positive Economics* (The University of Chicago Press, 1953) and *Milton Friedman's Monetary Framework* (The University of Chicago Press, 1976).

6. The foregoing has talked about 'equilibrium' rather than 'full' employment of resources. The latter is understood in the Classical system as any resources involuntarily unemployed would force down real wages until the market cleared.

7. A lucid exposition of the main ideas in New Classical analysis may be found in G. Davies, *Governments Can Affect Employment* (London: Employment Institute, 1985), Chapter 4. A more advanced treatment is C. L. F. Attfield, D. Demery and N. W. Duck *Rational Expectations in Macroeconomics* (Oxford: Basil Blackwell, 1985).

8. D. Begg, 'The New Classical Macroeconomics', *The Economic Review* May 1984, p. 28.

9. HM Treasury, 'Monetary Policy and the Economy', *Economic Progress Report*, no. 123, July 1980.

10. See also Treasury and Civil Service Committee, Session 1980/81, *Monetary Policy* (London: HMSO, 1981) HC 163–1, pp. xxx–xxxii. Evidence to this Committee expanded considerably on the exchange rate transmission mechanism.

11. Ibid, pp. xxxi–xxxii.

12. Had New Classical ideas been fully accepted the authorities would have engineered an immediate sharp cut in the money aggregates which, working through expectations, would have engendered (if the model was right) a rapid fall in the rate of nominal wage increases.

13. HM Treasury, *The British Experiment* Text of the Fifth Mais Lecture by the Rt. Hon. Nigel Lawson MP, Chancellor of the Exchequer, 18 June 1984. (Press Release).

14. See HM Treasury, *Economic Progress Report*, July 1980, for a discussion about the slight time trend in V.

15. Treasury evidence to the Treasury and Civil Service Committee, *Monetary Policy*, vol. II, Minutes of Evidence, p. 87, para. 10.

16. See HM Treasury, *The Financial Statement and Budget Report 1986/87* London, 1986, HC 273, Tables 1.2 and 6.5.

17. The contributions of the DCE subcomponents to the change in money stock are shown in the table opposite for the years 1981/82 to 1985/86. The definition of the money supply employed is £M3.

Formation of the money supply, £ Billions

	Unadjusted				
	1981/82	1982/83	1983/84	1984/85	1985/86
Public sector borrowing requirement	8.6	8.9	9.7	10.1	5.9
Less:					
Purchase of public sector debt by non-bank private sector	11.4	8.4	12.6	12.4	3.6
Plus:					
Lending in sterling	14.9	14.4	15.4	18.6	21.4
Domestic Credit Expansion	12.2	14.8	12.6	16.3	23.7
Less:					
External finance	1.1	3.1	2.7	1.8	2.7
Net non-deposit liabilities	1.5	1.9	2.3	2.7	1.9
Sterling M3	9.7	9.8	7.6	11.8	19.1

Source: *Bank of England Quarterly Bulletin*, vol. 26, June 1986, Table 11.3.

18. The 1984 FSBR introduced a target for narrow money, 'MO'; that for 1985 introduced a target for Money–GDP. All four targets for 1986 are shown below. Definitions of MO, £M3 and other monetary control candidates may be found in 'Changes to Monetary Aggregates and the Analysis of Bank Lending', *The Bank of England Quarterly Bulletin*, March 1984, pp. 78–83.

The 1986 MTFS Targets

					percentage
	1985/86	1986/87	1987/88	1988/89	1989/90
Money GDP[1]	9½ (8¼)	6¾	6½	6	5½
MO[2]	3½	2–6	2–6	1–5	1–5
£M3[2]	14¾	11–15	—	—	—
PSBR as per cent of GDP	2	1¾	1¾	1½	1½

Source: *Financial Statement and Budget Report 1986/87* (London, HMT, 1986) HC 273.
1.   Per cent change on previous financial year. The figure in brackets is adjusted for the coal strike. The figure for 1986/87 is a forecast; and in subsequent years the figures describe the Government's broad medium term objective. With GDP growth of 2 to 3 per cent the inflation target may be approximately inferred.
2.   1985/86: percentage change from mid-February to mid-February. 1986/87: target ranges. 1987/88 onwards: illustrative ranges for MO.

19. Another, more technical, criticism of actual performance against targets is contained in 'The Budget and the MTFS', *Barclays Review*, May 1986, pp. 49–52. When the MTFS was first conceived sales of public sector assets on the scale now obtaining were not envisaged. By

convention, these sales are treated as negative spending rather than as financing items. If they are added to the PSBR as financing items the following 'underlying' series emerges:

	1979/80	1980/81	1981/82	1982/83	1983/84	1984/85	1985/86
'Underlying' PSBR/GDP%	5.3	5.8	3.9	4.0	4.2	4.3	2.8
Normal PSBR/GDP%	4.8	5.6	3.4	3.2	3.2	3.1	1.6

Source: 'The Budget and the MTFS' *Barclays Review*, May 1986.

7 A Perspective on Cash Planning

1. Each year there are a number of more or less minor alterations to the definition of public expenditure which affect the continuity of the time series for cash spending. These are described fully each year in part II of the PEWP. For example, *PEWP 1987*, Cmnd. 56–II, pp. 26–28.
2. The full details may be consulted in the *FS & BRs* for 1982, 1983 and 1984.
3. See, for example, the *1983 PEWP*, Cmnd. 8789–I, para 5, p. 4.
4. In the Third Report from the Treasury and Civil Service Committee, Session 1982/83, *The Government's Expenditure Plans 1983/84 to 1985/86*, HC204, Appendix 2, p. 29, the Treasury estimate the effect in 1982/83, the first year of gradual abolition, to be about £¼ billion.
5. See Second Report from the Treasury and Civil Service Committee, Session 1985/86, *The Government's Economic Policy: Autumn Statement*, HC57, Appendix 4, Table 2, p. 49.
6. A point made by A. Likierman, 'Squaring the Circle: Reconciling Predictive Uncertainty with the Control of Public Expenditure in the UK', *Policy and Politics*, vol. 14, July 1986, p. 292.
7. See R. Robinson, 'Restructuring the Welfare State: An Analysis of Public Expenditure, 1979/80 – 1984/85', *Journal of Social Policy*, vol. 15, 1986, p. 3.
8. Some commentators regard this as giving a better impression of the level of public spending. There are still some privatisation proceeds embedded in the data for departmental spending – for example, the proceeds of council house sales are netted off housing expenditure – and it might be appropriate to take these into account: the arguments for and against such a treatment are inconclusive. See 'Public Sector Finances', *Barclays Review* May 1986, pp. 49–52.
9. HM Treasury, *PEWP 1982* Cmnd. 8494–I, paras, 20–23, pp. 6–7; *Economic Progress Report*, No. 143, March 1982, p. 9 and no. 151, November 1982, p. 3; FS & BR, March 1984, p. 8; and *The Next Ten Years: Public Expenditure and Taxation into the 1990s* March 1984, part III.

10. R. W. R. Price, 'Public Expenditure: Policy and Control', *National Institute Economic Review*, November 1979.
11. Ibid. p. 71.
12. Central Statistical Office, *United Kingdom National Accounts, Sources and Methods* (London: HMSO, 1985), Chapter 5, p. 39 ff gives an outline of the methodology.
13. Presumably the difference is explained by unusually high public sector pay awards. These would have expanded cash spending compared with a smaller relative effect on the input-based data used to construct the constant price series in the GGFC deflator's denominator.
14. See HM Treasury, *PEWP 1986*, Cmnd 9702–II, p. 126.
15. R. Robinson, *Restructuring the Welfare State*; who uses: (1) DOE, *Housing and Construction Statistics*; (2) DES *Handbook of Education Unit Costs 1982/83* (3) The all-items RPI and (4) Data released to the House of Commons Social Services Committee.
16. HM Treasury, *The Next Ten Years*.
17. *PEWP* 1987, Cmnd. 56–I, Table 1.10, p. 19.
18. See Annex 1 for a definition. Broadly, central and local government spending including gross debt interest, plus a few national accounts adjustments.
19. *FSBR* 1986, HC273, para 1.04, p. 5.

Conclusion

1. HM Treasury, *The Management of Public Spending*, para. 73 (emphasis added).
2. Rt. Hon. John MacGregor MP, 'Managing To Get Better Value For Money' 7 July 1986. Treasury press release of presentation to *Public Finance Foundation Seminar on Getting Value for Money in Business and Government*.
3. HM Treasury, *Output and Performance Measurement in Central Government: Progress in Departments* (London: HMT, February 1986), Annex B, p. 5.
4. See, for example Department of the Environment, *MINIS 6: Directorate Statements*, Parts 1–7, (London: DOE, December 1984–March 1985).
5. Chancellor of the Exchequer, *Progress in Financial Management in Government Departments* (London: HMSO, July 1984) Cmnd. 9297, p. 2 and Departmental chapters.
6. HM Treasury, *PEWP 1986*, Cmnd. 9702–I p. 26; and *The Management of Public Spending*, para. 59.
7. *3rd Report from the Treasury and Civil Service Committee*, 10 February 1986, p. xv.
8. Rt. Hon. John MacGregor MP, 'Managing to Get Better Value for Money', para. 6.22.
9. For example, a 5 per cent cash increase in spend with a 5 per cent

GDP deflator translates into constant spending in terms of what resources would buy in the economy generally.

10. *3rd Report from the T&CSC*, 10 February 1986, Q. 133, p. 21.
11. R. Robinson, 'Restructuring the Welfare State: An Analysis of Public Expenditure, 1979/80–1984/85', *Journal of Social Policy*, vol. 15, 1986.
12. See the timetable in HM Treasury, *Supply Estimates 1986/87. Summary and Guide*, (London: HMSO, March 1986) Cmnd. 9742.
13. Ibid.
14. Ibid., p. 7. The NAO paper *Financial Reporting to Parliament*, (London: HMSO, 1986) HC576, is largely concerned with this theme.

Index

adversarial planning 19–21
affordability 7, 11
aggregation problem in CBA 44
agriculture 37, 108
Anderson, L. G. 112
Armstrong Report 23, 109, 110
arts and libraries 110
Attfield, C. L. F. 115
Autumn Statement 17, 18, 19,
    23–4, 30, 31, 73, 102

*Bank of England Quarterly
    Bulletin* 116
Barclays Review 116–17
Barnett, J. 37, 111
baseline (PES) 13–15, 21
Begg, D. 64, 115
'beggars' sores' 109
bilaterals 16, 17, 18, 19, 36–17
'bleeding stumps' 19
borrowing 1, 2, 19, 30, 102, 107
Bridges, Lord 111
Bruce Gardyne, Lord 109
Budd, A. 57, 114
Budget 5, 8, 14, 18, 22, 25, 30,
    53, 67–9

Cabinet 3, 7, 14–17, 20, 21, 33,
    36
Cabinet Office 109
capital consumption 88
cash limits 6, 8–9, 11, 59
cash planning 7, 9–12, 25, 59–70,
    71–5, 77–80, 84–5
Castle, Lady 36, 109
Central Policy Review Staff 42,
    112

Central Statistical Office 107, 118
Chancellor of the Exchequer 3, 5,
    11, 15, 17, 23, 30, 42, 66, 73
Chief Secretary to the
    Treasury 15, 16, 17, 82, 84
civil service manpower 25
classical theory 49, 60–4
coal strike 75, 77
Colvin, P. 96, 101
Conservative administration 5, 7,
    37, 42, 50, 52
constant prices 6, 7, 25, 28, 59,
    60, 76, 102, 105
contingency reserve 9, 88
Cooper, Sir F. 111
cost–benefit analysis 42–4, 83,
    96–101
cost-effectiveness analysis 43, 83
crowding out 63
Customs and Excise 84

Davies, G. 53, 55, 112, 115
debt interest 87, 88, 89
defence 29, 37, 96
demand-led spending 13, 102,
    107
demand management 5, 39, 48,
    49, 58, 59
Demery, D. 115
Department of Economic
    Affairs 51–2
Department of Energy 19
Department of the
    Environment 109, 118
devaluation 51
domestic credit expansion 67
Duck, N. W. 115

economy, efficiency,
    effectiveness   82, 103, 106
equity   36, 45
Estimates   5, 6, 31, 32, 39, 81, 85–
    6, 107
Estimates, Summary and
    Guide   31, 85, 105
European Community   37, 103,
    108
exchange rate policy   53
exchange rate transmission
    mechanism   65
external financing limits
    (EFLs)   19, 31, 103

Financial Management
    Initiative   29, 82–4, 103, 108–
    9
Financial Statement and Budget
    Report   30, 67, 69, 104
financial transfers   2, 7–8, 25, 39,
    76, 78, 79, 107
fiscal policy   6, 50, 66, 67
Fisher's equation of
    exchange   61–2, 65, 66
forecasts   4, 6, 13, 14, 15–6, 17,
    63
Friedman, M.   62–3, 65, 115
futures markets   56, 104

GDP   1, 2, 39, 52, 53–4, 57, 66,
    88, 89, 104
GDP deflator   25, 74–7, 85, 89,
    110
general government final
    consumption deflator   76–8
General Practitioner
    payments   108
gilt-edged securities   67, 102, 104
Goldman, Sir S.   111
grants   8, 18, 76, 87, 88
Green Paper on tax burdens   33,
    110

Ham, C.   111
Harrison, A.   108
Heald, D.   11, 95, 108, 110
Healey, D.   111

health authorities   84
Heclo, H.   109, 111
Henley, Sir D.   111
Hennessy, P.   112
Home Office   37
hospitals   42
housing improvement grants   102

incomes policy   8, 66, 76
incremental budgeting   40, 46–7
indicative planning   48, 56–7
inflation   2, 6, 7, 8, 9, 10, 23, 49,
    51, 59, 64–5, 66, 68–9, 75, 84,
    107
inner cities   45
input–output relationship   29, 31
Institute for Fiscal Studies   23
Institute of Public Sector
    Management   34
interest rates   6, 13, 14, 49, 63, 64,
    66–7, 104

Jenkins, S.   108, 109

Keynesian theories   48–50, 52, 58,
    63, 70
Klein, R.   114

Labour administration   50, 52
labour market   23, 49, 57, 60–1,
    65, 66
leased assets   19
Lewis, S.   108
Likierman, A.   20, 108, 109, 110,
    117
local authorities   6, 8, 18, 23, 25,
    29, 31, 73

MacGregor, J. Rt Hon.   118
McKenzie, G.   113
macroeconomic theories   4, 39–40
Mais lecture   66
manifesto commitment   37–8, 42
marginal physical productivity of
    labour   60
Meade, J. E.   114
Medium Term Financial

Strategy 30, 66–70, 73, 79, 80, 84, 116
Metcalf, D. 12
microeconomic policy 66
Middleton, Sir P. 111
Mishan, E. 112
Monck, N. 111
monetarism 40, 60–4
monetary gradualism 65
monetary policy 50, 64–5
monetary transmission
    mechanism 62, 65
money aggregates 66
Mooney, G. 112
Mountfield, P. 114
Mulley, F. 20

Nash, C. A. 112
national accounts 2, 67, 76, 89, 105, 107, 118
National Audit Office 28, 34
National Debt 88
National Health Service 29
national insurance benefits 76
national insurance
    contributions 23, 30, 31
National Insurance Fund 31, 85, 108
National Insurance Surcharge 73
national savings 102
nationalised industries 8, 19, 23, 25, 31, 103
NATO 37
natural level of employment 64
new classical theory 63–4, 65
normative planning 56
nuclear waste disposal 45

O'Donnell, A. T. 112
O'Higgins, M. 114
oligopolistic competition 3, 57
opportunity cost 2, 3, 43, 74, 85, 105
'Options for Reductions' 15
output measures 29, 83

Parliament 3, 6, 8, 13, 17, 18, 23, 31, 36, 45, 85

Pearce, D. W. 112
Peat, Marwick & Mitchell 109
pensions 38, 39
performance indicators 29
PES timetable 13–17
Peston, M. H. 113
Piachaud, D. 53, 55
Pierce, D. G. 115
Pliatzky, L. 42, 43, 111, 112
Plowden, Plowden system 5–6, 7, 11, 55
police pay formula 37, 108
Political and Economic Planning
    Group 57
Ponting, C. 20, 109
portfolio balance 62, 65
Price, R. W. R. 76, 118
prices and incomes policy 8
Principal Finance Officers 109
prior claims model 50–55
priorities 7, 21, 23, 33, 36–47, 82–4
privatisation 23, 74, 89, 108
public expenditure planning
    total 9, 10, 16, 17, 72, 74, 88–9, 105
Public Expenditure Survey
    Committee 21, 39, 105, 109
Public Expenditure White
    Paper 7–10, 17, 25–9, 71–2, 74, 78–9, 83, 85–6, 88, 105
Public Finance Foundation 82
Public Money 96
Public Sector Borrowing
    Requirement 67–70, 104, 105

rate poundages 18
rates 18, 31, 68, 85, 108
Rawlinson, Sir A. 111
rational expectations 60, 63–4
real terms 25, 74–5, 77–8, 84–5, 105
real wage 60–1, 64, 65
reduced requirements 14, 108
Redundant Mineworkers Payments
    Scheme 19
relative price effect 8, 75–8, 105

rents   31, 85, 108
resource allocation   3, 36
resource planning   48–55
retail price index   76, 77, 78
revaluation factor   9, 10, 11, 14
Rhoads, S. E.   112
Rhodes, T. E.   112
risk aversion   45
risk neutrality   44
Robinson, R.   77, 85, 117, 118, 119
RPI deflator   77
running costs   25, 83–4

Sandford, C. T.   113, 114
Saunders, P. & Associates   109
scale problem in CBA   44
schools   42, 84
Seammen, D.   111
Settle, R. F.   112
Sinden, J. A.   112
Sloman, A.   111
social security   108
Special Employment Measures   43–4
'Star Chamber'   16, 20, 41, 42
Steel, D. R.   95
Stibbard, P.   89, 95
Stock Exchange   104
supply side of economy   50, 56, 58
survey prices   6, 7, 9, 10, 11, 68, 84, 105–6

targets   9, 57, 66, 67, 68, 71–2, 82, 84–5
taxes   23, 30, 33–4, 68, 73, 79, 89, 102, 104, 105

transport   6, 29, 42, 77
Treasury and Civil Service Committee   18, 31, 33, 34, 42, 82, 103, 106, 109, 110, 111, 115, 117, 118, 119
Treasury Bills   102
Treasury role   36–42
Treasury staffing   41
'trilateral'   17
Tysome, P. J.   115

uncertainty   44, 56–7
unemployment   13, 14, 15, 49, 50, 65, 68
unions   11, 13
university student awards   108

value for money   82, 106
value of life   43
Vass, P.   110
VAT   88
velocity of circulation   61, 62
volume planning   6, 9, 10, 11
volume squeeze   7, 9, 10
vote-headings   5
votes   6

Ward, T.   73
Wass, Sir D.   111
Whitelaw, Lord   16
Wildavsky, A.   109, 111
willingness to pay   43, 44

Worrell, A. C.   112

Young, H.   111